His veil is His oneness since nothing veils Him other than Him.

AWHAD AL-DIN BALYANI (D. 1288)

TRANSPARENT BODY, LUMINOUS WORLD

The Tantric Yoga of Sensation and Perception

Rupert Spira

SAHAJA

SAHAJA PUBLICATIONS

PO Box 887, Oxford OX1 9PR
www.sahajapublications.com

Copyright © Rupert Spira 2024

First published by Sahaja Publications 2016
Second edition by Sahaja Publications 2021
Third edition by Sahaja Publications 2024

Designed by Rob Bowden

ISBN 978-1-7395378-9-0

CONTENTS

CONTENTS

ACKNOWLEDGEMENTS

The yoga meditations in *Transparent Body, Luminous World* were transcribed and selected from several hundred guided meditations that I have given at meetings and retreats in Europe and the USA since 2012.

Too many people have been involved directly or indirectly with the production of *Transparent Body, Luminous World* to thank individually, but I would especially like to express my deep gratitude to Ed Kelly and Linda Arzouni for the vision, love and dedication they have put into the making of this collection.

I would also like to thank Michele Pike, Will Wright and Regina Flanigan for their transcription of the meditations; Jacqueline Boyle and Rob Bowden for their help with editing and design; and Francesca Rotondella and Ruth Middleton for their assistance with all aspects of organisation.

As always, any expression of gratitude would not be complete without reference to my friend and teacher Francis Lucille, who passed on to me the flame of understanding and also encouraged me to find new, experiential pathways that come directly from silence, and to tailor them to the current circumstances. I would also like to express my gratitude to my companion, Ellen Emmet.

Finally, I would like to thank all those, many of whom remain unknown to me, whose love of truth and beauty have inspired these contemplations and drawn them out of me.

It is absurd to speak of that which cannot be spoken. How then does one share the invisible?

In *Transparent Body, Luminous World*, Rupert Spira gives us means that evoke this presence. Where mundane words fall short, the poet, the man of heart, as Abhinavagupta calls him, by his absence allows the direct perspective to speak.

Formerly a renowned potter, Rupert's talent is surely an agent of this surrender. For what does a potter do? He does nothing other than allow, and his hands and body are but the transparent breath that invites and enables the unknown to reveal itself. Subsequently, the unpredictable firing process further liberates the potter from any act of appropriation: who can predict what will come out of the kiln?

So it is with this collection of yoga meditations. The words emerge from silence, and although this creativity has its roots in the Tantric tradition of Kashmir Shaivism and the teachings of Jean Klein, one feels their utter freshness in this moment. Rupert's teacher, Francis Lucille, must also be thanked for having transmitted the essence of this tradition so clearly.

In reading these contemplations, one must disappear, along with all reason, expectation and hope. Only then does this flowering blossom within oneself.

Nothing new appears. As Meister Eckhart said of St. Paul, 'He rose from the ground and, with open eyes, saw nothing', and this nothingness was God. This non-objective experience, through which the reader feels his own absence, without being able to appropriate it in any way, is the perfume that is revealed in this work.

Éric Baret
May 2016

Translated from the French by Ellen Emmet

As a young adult my interest in truth or the nature of reality involved the study and practice of the non-dual tradition of Advaita Vedanta. I received the initial teaching in this tradition at Colet House in London from Shantananda Saraswati, at that time the Shankaracharya of the north of India, and through the writings of Ramana Maharshi, who was my constant companion during those years. This exploration reached its culmination when, in my mid-thirties, I met my teacher, Francis Lucille, who introduced me to the teachings of Atmananda Krishna Menon and, more importantly, directly indicated the ultimate reality of experience.

Until this encounter, my primary interest had been the recognition of my true nature, which I considered to be the height of the spiritual path. However, soon after we met, Francis also introduced me to the Tantric approach of Kashmir Shaivism, which he had learnt from his teacher, Jean Klein, who himself had brought it from India to the West towards the end of the twentieth century. As a result, I realised that the recognition of our true nature is a stage in but not the end of the spiritual path. The aim of this approach is to establish the non-dual understanding in all realms of experience. It involves a process of realigning the way we feel the body and perceive the world with the recognition of our true nature of eternal, infinite Awareness.

Many traditional and contemporary commentaries place the Tantric tradition in opposition to the Vedantic approach. As a student I was spared this conflict, for the two approaches were presented as inner and outer faces of the same complete teaching. It is in this spirit that *Transparent Body, Luminous World* presents the Tantric teaching in this collection. Although the purpose of this collection is to present a contemporary rendition of the Tantric approach to sensation and perception, I would like to place this approach in the context of the Vedantic path.

*   *   *

The essence of the Vedantic path involves an inversion of attention upon its source, which can be triggered by a question such as, 'Who am I?', 'What is it that is aware of my experience?', 'Am I aware?', 'From where do my thoughts come?', 'What element of experience cannot be removed from me?' or 'What is the essential, irreducible nature of the mind?' Such questions have the power to invite the mind away from its customary objects of interest – thoughts, images, feelings, sensations and perceptions – towards its source, the subjective experience of being aware, or Awareness itself. This enquiry culminates in Awareness's recognition of its own eternal, infinite nature.

This path is sometimes referred to as self-enquiry or self-investigation. However, these terms – translations of the Sanskrit term *atma vichara* – are potentially misleading. They imply an activity of the mind rather than, as Ramana Maharshi described it, a sinking or relaxing of the mind into 'the heart', that is, into its source of pure Awareness or Consciousness. The term may, therefore, be more accurately translated as 'self-abiding' or 'self-resting', and is the essence of what is known in various spiritual and religious traditions as prayer, meditation, self-remembering, Hesychasm in the Greek Orthodox Church, or the practice of the presence of God in the mystical Christian tradition.

In order to undertake this 'inward-facing' path, one first has to separate oneself from everything that is not inherent in one's essential being, which shines in each of our minds as the knowledge 'I' or 'I am'. To establish the presence and primacy of our essential identity of pure Awareness, we have to separate ourself from those aspects of experience that are not inherent in us: our thoughts, feelings, sensations and perceptions. In doing so, we arrive at the conclusion, 'I am nothing that can be thought, felt, sensed or perceived; that is, I am nothing, not a thing or any kind of objective experience. I am the ever-present witness of experience, but am not myself an object of experience.'

In the Vedantic tradition this path of separating oneself from everything that is superfluous to one's essential being of pure Awareness is often initiated by a process referred to as *neti neti* – 'I am not this, not this' – and leads to the recognition 'I am Awareness or Consciousness itself'. This recognition is not itself enlightenment (although it is often mistaken as such in contemporary expressions of the non-dual teaching), but it paves the way for it. A deeper exploration of the nature of Awareness is required, culminating in Awareness's recognition of its own eternal, infinite nature. In this recognition, no new knowledge is gained or experienced. Rather, previous beliefs are removed from Awareness, enabling its essential, indivisible, irreducible nature to stand revealed.

The beliefs that make Awareness appear to be temporary and finite, that is, that make Awareness appear to share the destiny and limits of the body, are referred to in the Vedantic tradition as 'ignorance'. Ignorance is not an object that obscures the nature of Awareness, but rather an activity of thinking and feeling. The cessation of this obscuring activity is the process through which Awareness ceases to hide itself from itself in the form of mind, and recognises itself as it is. The *neti neti* process is, therefore, a prelude to the deeper exploration of self-enquiry or self-investigation, leading to self-abidance or self-resting. In this self-abidance, Awareness is, in most cases gradually but occasionally suddenly, divested of its limitations and, at some point, stands revealed to itself as it essentially is.

*   *   *

Awareness's recognition of its own eternal, infinite nature is variously known in the spiritual traditions as enlightenment, awakening, illumination or the simple recognition of one's essential, self-aware being – its recognition of itself. It is the culmination of the Inward Path, the Path of Exclusion, the Path of Return, the Path of Discrimination, the Path of Knowledge, Jnana Yoga or, as it is known in the Zen tradition, the Great Death. This approach is sometimes referred to collectively as the Direct Path, in that the mind turns its knowing or attention directly towards its source, irrespective of the content or condition of objective experience. No preparation, manipulation or purification of the mind or body is required as a prerequisite to this approach. In fact, from the point of view of the Direct Path, the progressive approaches are considered preparations for this final stage of the inward-facing path.

All the highest spiritual teachings express the same essential understanding, because the nature of reality is not something that varies from culture to culture. However, the form of its expression arises out of the culture in which it is expressed. A teaching is conditioned, though not essentially changed, by the local and temporal traditions of that culture. The Direct Path is, in my opinion and experience, the one that is best suited to our age and culture, and it is made most explicit in the Vedantic path of self-investigation and self-abidance.

However, this turning away from the objective elements of experience – thoughts, feelings, sensations and perceptions – for the purpose of establishing the presence, primacy and nature of Awareness still leaves a distinction between Awareness and its objects. In some traditional expressions of the teaching, this distinction may inculcate a negative attitude towards objective experience, considering it a hindrance to Awareness's recognition of its own being. It is in this context that we find expressions such as 'the despicable body' or 'the filthy ego' in some traditional and even some contemporary non-dual texts. For the full integration of this new understanding into all realms of our lives, the relationship between Awareness and its objects must be fully explored, and eventually dissolved.

Even after the recognition of our essential nature of eternal, infinite Awareness, it is common for many of us to find a discrepancy between what we understand and what we feel. We may understand that everything appears in Awareness, is known by Awareness and is made of Awareness, and yet we may still feel the body as something solid, dense, limited and located. Likewise, and as an inevitable corollary to this feeling, we may perceive the world as something that is separate and at a distance from ourself. Thus, our thoughts may be more or less free of the separate self, but our feelings and perceptions, and subsequent activities and relationships, may betray the residues of an apparently separate self still present in the deeper, more hidden layers of experience. The yoga meditations presented in this collection are aimed at dissolving this discrepancy.

This approach, which I call the Tantric Yoga of Sensation and Perception, starts with the recognition of our true nature and proceeds from there to fully explore the relationship between Awareness and objective experience. Although this relationship is implicit in the Vedantic tradition, it was made explicit in the Tantric traditions, particularly that of Kashmir Shaivism. Ramana Maharshi would sit for many hours in silence with his students, and the exposure and dissolution of these feelings would be brought about in this silence. In the Tantric traditions, of which this Yoga of Sensation and Perception is a contemporary expression, a more proactive approach is taken to exploring the feeling of separation in the body.

Thus, the two traditions of Vedanta and Kashmir Shaivism are complementary aspects of a complete approach to the exploration of experience, and not, as we so often find in scholastic commentaries on these two traditions, at odds with each other. Unfortunately, many contemporary Western expressions of the Tantric tradition are not sufficiently adapted to the culture in which they now find themselves and, as a result, the form of these teachings is often adhered to at the expense of their meaning.

In the cultures in which these teachings originated, their forms were tailored to the requirements of the people at hand, evolving and changing spontaneously, and always developing new pathways that corresponded intimately with their questions, difficulties and resistances. As such, the true Tantric tradition was a living, growing flame that was passed on from generation to generation, not a series of codified practices that could be disseminated by teachers and mechanically applied by students. In our culture, in the absence of this living tradition, a surrogate tradition of dogmas, codes and practices, still redolent of its countries of origin, masks the true teaching with elements that are foreign to the culture in which it now finds itself. This shrouds the teaching in an air of mystery, obscurity and esotericism, which the seeking ego mistakes for profundity and authenticity, and in which it takes refuge.

*   *   *

The Tantric path, of which the meditations presented in this collection are a contemporary expression, involves a turning towards experience. It is an exploration of objective experience in the light of our enlightened understanding, rather than a turning away from experience in favour of its background of pure Awareness, as is the case in the Vedantic approach. If the Vedantic path is the path from 'I am something' – a body and mind – to 'I am nothing', the Tantric path could be said to be the path from 'I am nothing' to 'I am everything'. If the Vedantic path is one of exclusion or discrimination, the Tantric path is one of inclusion or love. In the Zen tradition the Vedantic path is known as the Great Death, the Tantric path as the Great Rebirth.

This path of inclusion or love involves a realignment of feelings, sensations, perceptions, activities and relationships with the recognition of our eternal, infinite nature of pure Awareness. It is the second stage of the spiritual process, in which we return to the objective realm of experience, having already recognised our true nature. It is the path in which the residues of the separate self in the body are gradually exposed by, surrendered to and, in time, dissolved in the light of Awareness. It is an invitation to the body to be felt and the world to be perceived in a way that is consistent with the understanding that our true nature of eternal, infinite Awareness is the sole and ultimate reality of all experience. We do not want to simply *know* that I am ever-present, unlimited Awareness; we want to *feel* it, and we want to live in a way that is consistent with this feeling-understanding in all realms of experience.

The way we think, feel, act, perceive and relate has been conditioned for decades by the fundamental presumption of our world culture that our essential identity of Awareness is a temporary, finite entity that lives in and shares the limits and destiny of the body. This apparent mixture of Awareness and the limitations of the body gives rise to the belief and, more importantly, the feeling of being a temporary, finite entity or self. Being temporary, the apparently separate self or ego fears death or disappearance; being finite, it feels incomplete, and thus suffers from a chronic sense that something is missing.

These two feelings – the fear of death and the sense of lack – are the two elements that define the apparently separate self around whom most people's lives revolve, and on whose behalf our fears, desires, insecurities, neuroses and anxieties arise. The separate self is not an entity; it is an activity – the activity of thinking, feeling, acting, perceiving and relating on behalf of an imaginary, temporary, finite consciousness. That activity has been rehearsed for decades, and it does not come to an end with the recognition of our true nature. The source of that activity comes to an end, but its effects in the way we feel, act, perceive and relate continue. In other words, the feeling of separation in the body outlives enlightenment, in the same way that picking a flower cuts it off from its source of nourishment in the earth but doesn't bring it to an immediate end.

The deeper feelings that are the core of the separate self are often laid down early in childhood and, being too painful to face or bear, are buried in the body. They lie there, layer upon layer, below the reach of rational thought, as a network of tensions and feelings that betray themselves later in life as strategies of resistance and avoidance, frequently at odds with our deepest love and understanding.

Long after the recognition of our true nature, this great well of feelings can remain just below the surface of our waking-state experience, but susceptible to the slightest provocation in our relationships and circumstances. These are not just temporary, local feelings that arise in response to circumstances, such as, 'I am upset by this or irritated by that'. They are the subtler, chronic feelings that seem to pervade our experience, such as the feeling of being unlovable, unworthy, ashamed, afraid, inadequate or guilty. These feelings are buried below the threshold of rational thought and are beyond its reach, and reside, as a result, as a network of sensations in the body. It is as a result of this network of sensations that, in spite of our genuine understanding to the contrary, we still feel solid, dense, limited, separate and located.

It was in relation to such feelings that the Zen master, when asked on his deathbed how things were going, responded, 'Everything is fine, but my body is having a hard time keeping up!' The Zen master, in his humility and honesty, recognised that whilst his mind was clear there were still some residues left in the body that had not yet caught up with his profound realisation. This is the situation in which most people on the non-dual path find themselves. Carl Jung is supposed to have said of Ramana Maharshi that he was 'like a white spot on a white piece of paper'. However, most of us are various shades of grey!

*   *   *

Is it absolutely necessary to undertake the second stage of the process, this Tantric Yoga of Sensation and Perception? No, it is not required for the recognition of our true nature. The recognition of our true nature requires only Awareness's knowing of its own being and is independent of the content or quality of the mind or body. It is between Awareness and itself. However, if we want to access the peace and fulfilment that are inherent in our true nature of pure Awareness, and live and express this in life, that is, in our activities, relationships and perceptions, then yes, it is necessary to undergo this second part of the process.

In this yoga, the distinction between Awareness and its objects, which was effected in order to establish the presence, primacy and nature of

Awareness, is dissolved. In fact, it is not dissolved; it was never real to begin with. However, under normal circumstances our true nature of ever-present, unlimited Awareness is so completely lost in or merged with the objects of experience as to seem to have become limited by and, therefore, identical to them.

In the path of self-enquiry, Awareness is separated from its objects, and returns, as it were, to itself and recognises itself as it is. In the Tantric Yoga of Sensation and Perception, Awareness turns again towards the objects of experience. There is then a progressive infiltrating, pervading or saturating of the objects of knowledge and experience with the peace and happiness that are inherent in Awareness's knowing of its own being. That is, instead of Awareness being merged with experience, experience is merged in Awareness.

In ignorance, I, Awareness, seem to share the destiny and limits of the body and thus seem to be identical with it. In wisdom or understanding, Awareness recognises its own eternal, infinite being. In love, the body is known to share the qualities of Awareness and is felt, as such, to be open, empty, transparent, light, loving and intimately connected with all others and its environment.

One following the Vedantic path, or the Path of Discrimination, starts with 'I am not this, I am not this' and discovers the presence and primacy of Awareness, which is then, in the process of self-abidance, relieved of its apparent limitations and stands revealed as eternal and infinite. On the Tantric path, having discovered our essential nature of eternal, infinite Awareness, we no longer say, 'I am *not* this; I am *not* this'; rather, we say, 'I *am* this; I *am* this'. We turn towards experience, not away from it. We stand knowingly as the open, empty, transparent, loving presence of Awareness and allow experience fully into ourself, facing it with unconditional openness.

This is no longer something we have to do or practice. It is our nature. This unconditional openness to all experience is what we are, not what we do. We allow all experience – particularly those experiences that in the past we would have been motivated to avoid through the use of substances, activities, states of mind and relationships – to come fully into ourself. We stay with experience throughout all its permutations, thus allowing it to be gradually and progressively permeated and saturated with the light of Awareness, until in time all experience is revealed at an experiential level as a modulation of that. All experience is like a current in the ocean of Awareness.

The density and solidity of the body and the otherness of the world are penetrated and suffused with the light of pure knowing, God's infinite being, and are gradually outshone by it. The body becomes impersonal like the world, and the world becomes intimate like the body. At some point, there is a feeling-understanding that there is only God's infinite being, and everything is that. As the Sufis say, 'There is only God's face.'

The two paths of Vedanta and Tantra, in the forms in which they are presented in this collection, are not two opposing paths competing for the ultimate truth. They are complementary approaches which, divested of the cultural packaging that has alienated so many people from the simplicity and immediacy of the Great Tradition, provide our generation with an experiential path that stands up to the scrutiny of reason and includes all aspects of experience. It is a path that is thus well adapted to the requirements of the twenty-first century.

Rupert Spira
March 2016

MEDITATIONS

A companion audiobook of these meditations is available
at www.rupertspira.com and audiobook retailers.

EXPLORING THE TRUE EXPERIENCE OF THE BODY

In most of the great spiritual traditions there are two complementary paths, the inward-facing path and the outward-facing path. The inward-facing path is based on the mind's recognition of the essential nature of its own experience. The mind notices that all it knows is its own experience. That is, the mind notices that all it ever knows or comes in contact with is itself: thinking, imagining, feeling, sensing, perceiving. Everything that is known by the mind takes place in the mind.

If everything appears in the mind, then everything that appears must share the essential nature of the mind. Therefore, in order to know the essential nature of anything, such as the body or the world, the mind must first know its own nature. The mind's knowledge of things is only as good as its knowledge of itself. As the Sufis say, 'Whoever knows their self knows their Lord.' That is, whoever knows the essential nature of the mind knows the ultimate reality of the universe.

This recognition that in order to know the nature of anything we must first know the nature of our own mind is a pivotal moment in our lives and triggers a revolution. It is this recognition that the painter Paul Cézanne was referring to when he said, 'A single carrot freshly observed will trigger a revolution.'

This recognition triggers the ultimate revolution, and I mean 'revolution' literally. It triggers a turning around of the mind. The mind recognises that in order to know the nature of anything, it must first know the nature of itself. Therefore, there can be no higher endeavour than to explore and discover the nature of the mind. That is, there can be no greater endeavour for the mind itself than to discover its own nature.

With this simple recognition, the mind turns around – the ultimate revolution – and it questions its own reality: 'Who am I? What am I? What is my essential nature? What is the nature of the knowing with which all knowledge and experience is known?'

The mind recognises that thinking is not inherent in it. It is not essential, therefore cannot be what mind essentially is. Feeling, sensing and perceiving are not essential to the mind. They come and go, but the mind is always present throughout all these changes, therefore they cannot be inherent in what it is.

The mind asks itself, 'What am I? What is my essential, irreducible, unchanging nature?' and this question triggers the inward-facing path. When I say 'inward' I don't mean inwards towards the body; I mean inwards towards the source or the essential nature of the mind.

This Direct Path of self-investigation has been the essential ingredient of the traditional Vedantic teachings for many centuries. However, because many people found it too difficult, the teachers in this tradition elaborated other, more progressive approaches and, as a result, this direct approach fell into disuse and obscurity. It was only resurrected by Ramana Maharshi and Atmananda Krishna Menon, amongst others, in the middle of the last century. They reformulated this approach for a new generation.

They brought this Direct Path of self-investigation out of the esoteric schools, where it was given to initiates who had done thirty or forty years of preparatory practices, and made it available to everyone. They felt that our world culture had reached a sufficient level of maturity to enable this direct approach to be made available to everyone, not just the initiates in ashrams and monasteries. I feel very much the same way, that our age is ripe for the Direct Path. We no longer need to go via an object to our true nature.

*   *   *

So, as the mind turns its attention, or turns the light of its knowing, upon itself it embarks on what we could call the return journey, the return to the source from which it initially arises. In doing so, the mind is, in most cases, gradually and progressively relieved of its limitations. Occasionally this happens suddenly, and we are all familiar with the few stories of cases in which this liberation from the limitations of the mind happened suddenly.

But this is very rare, and we shouldn't expect it to happen in our case like that. In almost all cases, it is a gradual and progressive liberation of the mind from its self-imposed limitations.

Why do I say 'self-imposed limitations'? Because Awareness, or pure Consciousness, the source from which the mind arises, itself freely assumes the form of the finite mind. Nothing imposes the mind on Consciousness from the outside. It is infinite Consciousness that freely assumes the form of the finite mind, thereby limiting itself, in order to realise a part of the unmanifest potential that lies within it, in the form of the world.

So, the finite mind is not a mistake; it is not a problem. In Sanskrit the activity of the finite mind is sometimes referred to as *avidya*, which is usually translated as 'ignorance'. However, it is ignorant only in the sense that it involves the ignoring or veiling of the reality of the mind, just as a movie involves the veiling of the screen.

In that sense, mind is sometimes said to be ignorance, but the term ignorance in this context does not carry the connotation that it does in the English language, where ignorance is analogous with stupidity. However, because of the association of ignorance with stupidity in English, the translation of the Sanskrit term *avidya* as ignorance has given rise to the belief that objective experience – the mind, the body and the world – is somehow wrong or a mistake. This led to many body-negative or body-denying attitudes in some traditional expressions of the Advaita or non-dual teaching.

The finite mind is not a mistake. Consciousness doesn't make mistakes; it is complete freedom. Consciousness assumes the form of the finite mind out of its freedom, limiting itself in order to give birth to manifestation in the form of the world.

However, manifestation comes at a price. Consciousness limits itself in order to manifest its infinite potential in the form of the world, but in doing so ends up as a temporary, finite consciousness – the separate self, mind or ego – inside the very world which it has created, just as a spider spins a web out of herself and then becomes entangled in the web. Consciousness gives birth to the world within itself and then becomes a separate subject of experience in that world, from whose point of view that world is now known.

Consciousness gets lost in its own creativity. It seems to become a self in the world. In the form of that temporary, finite self or ego, Consciousness then has to trace its way back home to discover its true nature again, just as the spider has to extricate itself from the web in which it now finds itself entangled.

This tracing back of the finite mind to its infinite source of pure Consciousness is the inward-facing path, the path of self-investigation. 'Who am I? What am I? What is the nature of the knowing with which I know all experience? What is it that is aware of my experience?' All these questions are triggers that effect this turning around or revolution of the mind, in which it gradually returns to its source and, in doing so, is progressively relieved of its self-imposed or self-assumed limitations.

This return of the mind to its source involves a relaxation of the mind, a sinking of the mind; it doesn't just happen in a moment. As Jalāl ad-Dīn Rumi said, 'Flow down and down and down, in ever-widening rings of being.' Ever-widening, that is, as the mind flows down, or back and back and back into its source, it widens: it gradually loses its limitations as it sinks into its source.

As the mind sinks deeper and deeper into its source, it simply rests there. What began as a process of self-investigation ends up simply in self-abidance, mind resting in its source. It is in this self-resting that the mind is relieved of its limitations.

If we want a metaphor for this self-resting or self-abidance, we could imagine a dirty dishcloth. In order to clean the dishcloth we place it in a basin of warm, soapy water and scrub it. The scrubbing removes much of the dirt, but the deeply ingrained stains remain. In order to remove these more deeply ingrained stains we simply leave the dishcloth soaking in the warm, soapy water. It is this soaking that effects the cleaning of the deeper layers of dirt. Self-abidance is the soaking of the mind in its source of pure Consciousness.

The Sanskrit term *atma vichara*, which is normally translated 'self-enquiry' or 'self-investigation', has two parts to it. The first part is a process of questioning in which there is something for the mind to do: 'What is the nature of my self? Who am I? What is the nature of the knowing with which I know my experience?'

In time, this activity becomes subtler and subtler until, in the end, there is no more for the mind to do other than to rest its source of pure Consciousness, which is the experiential answer to these questions. It is in this self-resting or self-abiding that the mind is relieved of its limitations. That is why the larger part of the path of self-investigation is really self-abidance or self-resting.

This is what Ramana Maharshi was referring to when he said that the highest meditation is simply to be – not to do anything with the mind, not to direct the mind towards anything, just to leave the mind resting or abiding in its source, the self-resting of the mind.

*   *   *

So that is a brief summary of the inward-facing path, and we find this path in some form in nearly all the spiritual traditions, whether it is called self-investigation, self-enquiry, self-abidance, the practice of the presence of God, as the Christian mystics call it, self-remembering, as the Russian philosopher P. D. Ouspensky called it (although it was very often mis-understood by his students), prayer, meditation, focusing on the 'I am', or simply giving our attention to the feeling of being.

This effortless form of meditation, which is in fact a non-practice, is the ultimate meditation, the highest form of prayer, because it is the only form of meditation that doesn't require an object for the mind to focus on. It doesn't require a mantra, a teacher, the breath, the space between breaths, a flame, and so on. All of these are more or less subtle objects to-wards which the mind directs itself. The Direct Path gives the mind no object to focus on. It is the opposite of focusing; it is the relaxing or sink-ing of the mind into its source. It is a sinking of the mind into the heart, as Ramana Maharshi said.

At some point there is the revelation that the essential nature of the mind is transparent, empty, ever-present Consciousness. It doesn't appear, it wasn't born, it doesn't move or change or age, it is not going to die or dis-appear, and it has no limits. Being unlimited, there is only one infinite Consciousness. Each of our finite minds is precipitated within and made of the same infinite Consciousness. Therefore, at the deepest level, all of our minds are connected. We are literally one. That experience, the recog-nition of our shared being, is commonly called love.

That is the great revelation, the culmination of the inward-facing path, which is referred to as illumination, or awakening, or enlightenment. All of these are rather exotic terms that for most of us have various cul-tural associations that make them sound as if they are extraordinary experiences, only available to a few exceptional people. For this reason, I tend to avoid using such terms and just refer to the simple knowing of our own being as it is, its knowing of itself in us.

When this recognition takes place, the mind is not instantly relieved of all its old habits. The mind has been rehearsing its habits for many decades, and they do not disappear immediately on the recognition of our true nature. Habits last. Habits of thinking are relatively quick to disappear. Once we see our father tiptoeing out of our bedroom at three o'clock on Christmas morning, leaving a stocking on the end of our bed, our belief in Father Christmas ends instantly.

So, ideas and beliefs are relatively quick to realign themselves with our new recognition of infinite Consciousness, or its recognition of itself. However, our feelings are not so quick to realign themselves. It is possible in theory for our feelings to be cleaned up overnight, but it is very rare, and in almost all cases the feeling of being temporary, finite, separate and limited outlives the recognition of our true nature and continues to express itself in the way we feel the body, and in our postures, movements, activities and relationships.

It is this discrepancy between what we understand and what we feel that is responsible for so many questions that people have: 'I have been studying and practicing non-duality for forty years and clearly understand it, and yet still feel that something is missing, and still find myself behaving in ways that betray the presence of a separate self lurking in my experience, despite my genuine understanding that I am not a temporary, finite, located, separate self.' Or, 'I continually find that, in spite of my non-dual understanding, my feelings sabotage my behaviour, friendships and intimate relationships.'

This conflict between what we understand and what we feel is due to the echo of separation still reverberating in the body. The feeling of separation has not yet been flushed out of the body, although it has to a large extent been flushed out of the mind. This discrepancy between our ideas and feelings is also an explanation for a phenomenon that we see in many teachers and which gives rise to many questions: 'How come so-and-so can speak with such genuine understanding and clarity and yet behave in inconsistent ways?'

We have in our culture the idea that a teacher is a kind of ideal person whose beliefs, feelings, activities and relationships are absolutely perfect.

There may be a few people like that – as Carl Jung said of Ramana Maharshi, 'He was a white spot on a white piece of paper' – but most of us are various degrees of pale grey spots on a white sheet of paper.

I do not say this to legitimise inappropriate behaviour in those who speak or write about the non-dual understanding, but rather to make it clear that the feeling of separation in the body outlives the recognition of our true nature and, in doing so, to pave the way for the Tantric Yoga of Sensation and Perception that we are interested in here. There is a story of a Zen master who was asked by one of his students on his deathbed, 'How are things for you now?' The Zen master replied, 'Everything is fine, but my body is having a hard time keeping up.'

Everything was fine. His mind was open, spacious, clear, at peace, and yet there was this beautiful and humble acknowledgement in him that there were some corners of his experience, his feelings in the body, that had not yet caught up with his great and genuine understanding. This was not a failure on the part of the Zen master; it was just a very human recognition that the body/mind had not yet been completely colonised, saturated, permeated with his understanding.

*   *   *

So the approach to the body in these yoga meditations comes from the understanding that there is a further step after the recognition of our true nature, in which we encourage the body to be felt and the world to be perceived in a way that is consistent with our new non-dual understanding.

These yoga meditations, as I call them, are designed to do just this: to help and encourage the body liberate itself from feelings of density, limitation, location, heaviness, separateness. It is not a rational exploration. In other words, these yoga meditations don't use the clean, clinical lines of reasoning that we use in our conversations or dialogues. These lines of reasoning are very effective at exposing, uprooting and dissolving belief systems, but they do not touch our feelings. Our feelings lie below the threshold of rational thought and survive even the most astute, intelligent analysis.

It is for this reason that these yoga meditations proceed in non-rational ways, using visualisation and feeling rather than reason. Let me give you an example. Imagine we are a musician. We play the flute, violin, piano or guitar, and we prepare a piece of music for our teacher. Our teacher asks us to play it for her, but before we play it she asks us to imagine that we are performing it on our first night at Carnegie Hall, and to visualise and play the piece as if that were the case.

If we are a pianist we are playing one of the slow movements from one of Beethoven's piano sonatas, if we are a flautist or violinist we are playing a slow movement from one of the Bach partitas, and if we are a singer and guitarist we are playing a love song that we recently composed for our sweetheart. So we play the piece of music as if to an audience at Carnegie Hall, and our teacher listens and at the end says, 'Thank you. You played that perfectly.'

Now our teacher ask us to play the same piece of music again, but before we play it she asks us to imagine that we are in a room with our dearest and most intimate companion, and he or she is about to take a long journey, and we don't know if or when we will see each other again. Our teacher asks us to imagine that this piece of music is the last communication we are going to have with our friend, and then asks us to start playing.

So, we play the same piece of music. In both cases we play them note-perfect, but the quality of the two pieces of music is completely different. All we did was first visualise playing in front of an audience at Carnegie Hall and then in a room with our dearest and most intimate companion. Just that feeling-visualisation was enough to profoundly change the quality of our playing. That is the power of visualisation, feeling-visualisation, to re-orchestrate the body, to re-orchestrate our feelings, sensations and perceptions.

These yoga meditations work in a similar way. It is not necessary to analyse why there is a difference between playing at Carnegie Hall and to our most intimate companion. We don't need an explanation. The fact is that it works.

If we really want to be established in this understanding at all levels of our experience, a further investigation of the body and the world is important. When Atmananda Krishna Menon was asked, 'How do I know when I am established in my true nature?' he replied, 'When thoughts, feelings and perceptions can no longer take you away.'

He did not say when just thoughts can no longer take us away. It is not just when our thoughts are clearly aligned with the non-dual perspective but, more importantly, when our feelings and perceptions are fully

10

aligned, that we can say that we are really established in this understanding and that all aspects of our life – thoughts, feelings, perceptions, activities and relationships – are an expression of this understanding.

* * *

I suggest, to begin with, that we keep our eyes closed. The only reason for closing our eyes is that we are going to explore the experience of the body, not the experience of the world. We close our eyes just to temporarily shut out the vision of the world, which is not the focus of our attention at the moment. → *remember I am listen to these later*

Allow the experience of the body to come to your attention. I want to take some time to be sure that we all understand clearly what is meant by the phrase 'the experience of the body'. →

First of all, think about your body. Now, that series of thoughts is not the actual experience of the body; it is the experience of thought. Put those thoughts on one side. We're not going to be referring to them now.

Now take the image of your body, the image that you might see in the mirror or a photograph, or looking down at your body. Again, that is not the actual experience of the body. Put it on one side.

Now, what remains of our actual experience of the body? Whatever that is, is what I refer to as the experience of the body. It is simply a sensation or a network of sensations. By the word 'sensation' I mean something very specific.

Traffic sounds

The sound of traffic outside is not a sensation; it's a perception. Leave it alone. A thought or an image or a perception is not a sensation.

Go to the experience of the tingling of your face. That is a sensation. A headache is a sensation. The experience of hunger is a sensation. The tingling of our hands or the soles of our feet is a sensation.

Simply allow the sensation of the body to come to your attention. One way that sometimes helps us to be very clear that we stick only to the actual experience of the body is to imagine that we are a newborn infant. The reason for doing this is that a newborn infant doesn't have any thoughts or images of its body. The newborn infant is like a bundle of

think that this book is going to help me. Thank you.
I really need this. I really need this book.

pure sensitivity, pure experiencing. All it can do is experience. It has no idea what it is experiencing. For instance, the newborn infant has no idea that it is or has a body. All it feels is this tingling sensation or vibration appearing in this openness, in this field of experience.

So allow the experience of the body to come to your attention. See that our only experience of the body, if we don't refer to thought or memory, is the current sensation or vibration, and simply allow this tingling vibration to appear in the empty field of experience. Know nothing about it. Allow any lingering thoughts or images that may be attached to the sensation to fall away. They are not inherent in it; they are superfluous to it.

Notice that we are not actually doing anything to the body. We are not manipulating it or trying to change it in any way. We are simply contemplating it in a disinterested fashion, experiencing it as it is, prior to conceptualisation by thought.

Simply allow the sensation to be present in your experience as it is. There is nothing for thought to do.

Now ask yourself the question, 'What shape does this sensation have?'

Thought asks the question, but don't allow the questioning thought to trigger a series of other thoughts. Just let the thought initiate the investigation, and then explore the sensation itself. In order to discover what shape it is, we have to go to the edge of the sensation, if indeed we can find an edge.

So, a refinement of the question would be, 'Does this sensation have an edge or a border?'

Don't just take one look. Take your magnifying glass. Be detail orientated, and very sensitively scan the entire sensation, looking for an edge, a place where it ends, looking for a line that defines its shape.

*   *   *

Another tool that we can use to really help us explore the sensation itself is to imagine that we draw it on a piece of paper. So, in our imagination, we take out a sheet of white paper and a pencil. On our piece of paper we try to represent the experience of this sensation, referring only to our current, direct experience.

Remember, we are a newborn infant. We have never seen or thought about our body. We have no past to refer to. All we can refer to is the current, direct experience, and we try to draw that experience on our sheet of paper. What kind of marks do we make on the paper?

Be detail orientated. Go to the area that thought will subsequently label 'my head', and see that we have no actual experience of a head. We have no direct, experiential knowledge of a face, eyes, ears, a nose, a mouth or cheeks. All that we find there in our actual experience is a tingling, amorphous vibration. In our actual experience, we have no head as it is conceived by thought.

What kind of marks are we going to make on our piece of paper to represent this tingling vibration? On my drawing there are just clusters of dots. In some places the clusters are a little more intense, in others the dots disperse, and there are other areas on my drawing where there are simply large areas of empty white that represent where there is no sensation at all, just the empty field of experiencing.

Allow the chest and back to come to your attention. See, in fact, that we have no chest or back. All the newborn infant knows at this moment are clusters of sensation, vibrating more or less intensely in the empty field of experiencing.

Allow the belly and pelvic area and legs to come to your attention, but immediately drop the labels. Stay only with the raw, current, direct experience itself.

See clearly that the apparently well-defined edge of the body called 'my skin' is itself simply a tingling vibration. It is not a continuous membrane or envelope that contains the body. The skin itself, insofar as it is experienced, is an amorphous, tingling vibration. It is not a continuous membrane; it is just pockets of vibration, clusters of dots on the white page.

See clearly that the sensation of the body is not enclosed by a membrane. The so-called membrane of the skin is itself simply a sensation or vibration. That sensation has no edge to it. It is not enclosed or contained. It is just dots floating on the empty page.

Some of us may be experiencing pain. If that is the case, all we know of the pain is a slightly more intense sensation, and on our drawing this is represented by clusters of dots a little closer together. They may form a little dark patch in the middle of the page, but still it is just dots on the page. It is just sensation floating on the empty white page of experience.

Notice again that we are not touching the sensation; we are not manip- ulating our experience. We are simply allowing the body to reveal itself as it is in our actual experience, and in doing so we are allowing it to self- liberate itself from all the beliefs and feelings that have been superimposed upon it. We are not adding anything to the experience of the body; we are simply removing layers of belief and feeling.

Ask yourself the question, 'Does this sensation have an age?' Don't refer to thought or memory. We have no past to refer to; we have just been born. We are a field of pure experiencing, pure sensitivity. All we can do is experience the sensation in the moment.

Even to call it a sensation is too much. It is simply an amorphous, tin- gling, indefinable, unnameable vibration.

Does this sensation have a gender or a nationality?

*   *   *

Now ask yourself the question, 'Does this sensation have a weight?' Pay particular attention to the experience of weight. If the body is made out of something called 'matter', then it must weigh something, but if it is made out of something called 'Consciousness', then it cannot weigh anything.

Which is true in our experience? If we feel that our body weighs some- thing, then this feeling betrays the belief that it is made out of something called matter, and this is inconsistent with our understanding that all ex- perience appears in Consciousness, is known by Consciousness and is made of Consciousness.

So, go to that part of the sensation that seems to be evidence of weight, which for the most part is the contact area between our legs and the chair or floor. This part of the sensation is a little bit more intense than other areas. It is a part of our drawing where the black dots are more closely clustered together on the page.

It is true that the sensation is a little bit more intense here than, say, the sensation at the back of the head or the shoulders, where it is almost trans- parent unless we have a headache or a back ache. But just because the sensation is more intense, does that mean it is made out of something called matter? Does that mean that the sensation weighs something?

Ask yourself the question, 'How much does a sensation weigh?' Is a sensation something that we can put on the bathroom scales?

Feel the temperature of the air on your skin. Immediately drop the label and feel the very subtle sense of warmth. The feeling of warmth is just a sensation. All there is to the experience of warmth or cold is a sensation.

Ask yourself the question, 'How much does the experience of warmth weigh?' Obviously nothing. The experience of warmth or cold doesn't weigh anything.

Now ask yourself, 'What is it that makes me feel the sensation called "my legs on the chair or floor" is evidence of weight? What is it that makes me feel the sensation called "my legs on the chair or floor" is evidence of density, solidity, matter, whereas it is quite clear that the experience of warmth, which is just a slightly less intense sensation, weighs nothing and has no density or solidity to it?'

For the newborn infant, the only difference between the sensation of warmth and the feeling of its body lying in a cradle is one of intensity. These two experiences are both simply sensations, more or less intense but made out of exactly the same stuff, the same empty, transparent stuff, vibrating in the open field of experiencing, floating on the white page of experience.

Now ask yourself the question, 'Is there anything in my actual current experience, if I don't refer to thought or memory, that justifies my belief that I am sitting on a chair or a floor?' The thought that I am sitting on a chair or a floor presumes first of all that I am a body and, secondly, that this body is sitting on something called a chair or a floor, that is, something that is not me.

The newborn infant has no idea that it is or has a body. The newborn infant is simply a field of pure sensitivity, pure experiencing, and everything that is experienced is arising within this field. The newborn infant has no idea that this sensation or vibration is something called 'a body', nor does it know anything of an object or series of objects called 'the world'.

Allow the interface between the so-called body and the so-called chair or floor to come to your attention. Can we find a line there? Is there a clear distinction, as thought believes there is, between the sensation, called 'me', and the chair or floor, called 'not me'? Or is it one single, indivisible, homogenous sensation?

See in the intimacy and immediacy of your experience that the body is not sitting on a chair or floor, but rather that this tingling, amorphous, borderless vibration is suspended weightlessly in the empty field of pure experience.

If we want an image to aid this feeling, visualise a cloud floating weightlessly in the sky. This sensation is floating weightlessly in the open, empty sky of Awareness.

Visualise and feel that the edges of this cloudlike sensation bleed imperceptibly into the sky of Awareness. See that we cannot find a clear distinction between the cloudlike sensation and the open, empty sky of Awareness in which it is appearing. They merge and blend with each other.

*　*　*

Allow the experience of the breath to come to your attention. Lengthen and deepen the breath so that the inhale and exhale are three or four seconds, without forcing it.

Visualise and feel that on the inhale the breath seeps into the sensation of the body all over its entire porous surface. The breath fills up the sensation and then pours out of the sensation, all over its entire porous surface, into the empty space.

So we are not breathing through the nose. The entire so-called surface of the skin is our nose. It is like a piece of very fine, porous muslin, and we are breathing emptiness through this porous, permeable membrane into the sensation, filling up the sensation with the emptiness of the breath, and then the breath seeps out on the exhale in all directions, into the space all around.

First we visualise this, and then we drop the visualisation and simply feel it. Know and feel that the substance we are breathing into the sensation is not dead, inert stuff called 'air'. The newborn infant has no knowledge of air. The medium in which this sensation is appearing is not physical space filled with air. It is the field of pure experiencing, pure Consciousness, pure Awareness.

Feel that you are breathing empty Awareness into this tingling, amorphous, borderless sensation all over its entire porous surface, filling up the sensation with emptiness, and the emptiness then seeps out in all directions into the space all around.

Feel that the field of Awareness that we are breathing into the sensation is *loving*. It is the field in which our entire experience is contained, held, nourished, sustained. It is totally accepting, allowing, loving. Feel that we are breathing this loving substance in and out of the sensation.

Feel that on each inhale the sensation is progressively permeated and saturated with this empty, loving substance, and then on the exhale this empty, loving substance pours out of the sensation in all directions into the space around.

With each inhale, we allow this loving emptiness to penetrate more and more deeply into the sensation. The separate self, the 'me' feeling in the body, is like a network of sensations laid down, layer upon layer, each layer slightly more subtle than the one before, like a Russian doll. It takes time and several repeated attempts for this loving substance to fully infiltrate and permeate the density of 'me' feelings in the body.

If we are thinking, 'I don't want to do this', 'I can't do this', 'I don't know how to do this' or 'I've done this before', what we are really saying, without realising it, is, 'I want to remain a separate self. I don't want to be dissolved. I don't want to be expanded beyond my customary limits.'

Our resistance to this exploration is simply a justification for the apparent existence of the separate self. These resisting thoughts are simply verbal expressions of a deeper resistance in the body, the resistance of the separate self to being exposed and flushed out of its hiding places in the body. It is the separate self resisting exposure and dissolution, and justifying that resistance at a rational level.

If we find that there is any part of the sensation that resists being penetrated by this empty, loving substance of the breath, put that area under the microscope. Take extra time. Focus on that area, but no forcing. We simply invite the breath to penetrate more and more deeply into the density of the sensation.

Visualise this resistance like a little dark cloud suspended weightlessly in the open, empty sky of Awareness, and gently breathe this loving, empty substance in and out of it, all over its entire porous surface.

*   *   *

If there are any feelings that are triggered by this contemplation, notice the impulse to avoid the discomfort of these feelings. Be courageous. Turn towards the uncomfortable feeling and breathe loving emptiness in and out of it. Visualise and feel that the uncomfortable feeling is completely safe, held, nurtured, suspended in this loving, empty Presence.

Visualise and then feel that the sensation is filled up, permeated, saturated with this loving emptiness on the inhale, and on the exhale the sensation begins to expand into the space all around. The exhale carries the sensation out into the space in all directions, all over its entire porous surface.

With each inhale the sensation is more and more deeply penetrated, and with each exhale it is more and more widely dispersed into the space all around. The cloud is dispersing and dissolving in the sky.

Cease controlling your breathing or focusing on the sensation. Stop doing anything in particular. Simply allow the entire realm of experience to be present in the empty, loving field of Awareness. Include not just the sensation but thinking, hearing, feeling, imagining and seeing, if our eyes are open.

See that all experience appears in the same open, empty, allowing field. Each of these – thinking, imagining, feeling, sensing, seeing, hearing, touching, tasting, smelling – is just a cloud appearing in the same sky of Awareness, known by the sky of Awareness, made of the sky of Awareness, different in its name and form but each a modulation of the same transparent, empty Presence.

All objects and selves share their being. They borrow their seeming existence from the only one that truly is: infinite Consciousness, known commonly as 'I', known religiously as God's infinite being. Everything is only that.

THE SELF-AWARE FIELD OF CONSCIOUSNESS

If we believe and feel that 'I am the body', then it will seem to us that part of our experience takes place on the inside and part of our experience on the outside. It will seem as if experience is divided into two essential parts: an inside part made out of mind, and an outside part made out of matter.

The inside part – thoughts, images, feelings, sensations – we consider to be 'me'. The outside part – perceptions of the world – we consider to be 'not me'. So it is this 'I am the body' belief and feeling that is responsible for the essential division of experience into two separate parts: self and other, mind and matter.

The reason why science finds it so impossible to give up its materialist paradigm is because the scientists involved are deeply wedded to the 'I am the body' belief. However, if we understand and feel that 'I am Awareness', then it becomes obvious to us that *all* experience takes place on the inside, that is, takes place in Awareness.

I know that for some of you this is obvious, but let's just go very slowly for those of us for whom it is not yet completely obvious. I suggest you start with your eyes closed.

Allow a thought or a series of thoughts to arise, and feel that those thoughts appear 'in me'. None of us have any problem with that. Everybody, even from a conventional point of view, understands and feels that their thoughts appear inside themselves. So just listen to the sound of your thoughts. Feel that those sounds take place inside you. Don't be interested in the content of your thoughts. Just listen to them as abstract sounds, as you might listen to music.

Now listen to whatever sounds are taking place in what, from a conventional point of view, is considered to be 'outside me'. Just listen to the sounds without attributing any content or meaning to them.

Go back and forth from the sound of your thoughts to the sound of this voice. Just go back and forth, visiting each one, until it is completely obvious to you that both these sounds appear in the same space.

You direct your attention to the sound of your thoughts, then you direct your attention to the sound of this voice, or whatever sounds are present. As you go back and forth between the two, see if your attention ever crosses a border. See if your attention ever leaves Consciousness. See if your attention ever leaves 'the inside of me' and enters a space called 'the outside world'. Be very specific. Try to find that border, if indeed it is there, the border where your attention leaves Awareness and enters a realm called 'the world outside Awareness'.

Discover in this way that the border between 'the inside of me' and 'the outside of me' is not there. If we believe 'I am the body', then the border is the skin. But if we understand 'I am Awareness', then there is no border. Attention never leaves Awareness. The border is on the map, but it is not in the territory.

It's like walking from England into Wales. You never find the line on the ground that distinguishes the two. It's the same thing here. The border between the inside and the outside of experience, the inside and the outside of 'me', is never found. Attention never leaves Awareness.

*   *   *

Now give your attention to the tingling sensation behind the eyes. That sensation, even from a conventional point of view, is taking place in 'me'. Now place your hand on your chair. A new sensation arises, and from a conventional point of view this sensation is a sensation of something outside of 'me', made out of something other than 'me', called 'matter'.

Now, with your attention again, go back and forth between these two sensations, the sensation labelled 'tingling behind the eyes' and the sensation labelled 'hand on chair'. Drop the labels; just experience the raw, unnameable sensation.

Ask yourself the question, 'Do these two sensations appear in the same space of Awareness, in the same space of myself? Or does one sensation appear in me and another sensation appear in "not me", that is, the world?'

Don't just be interested in the sensations; be interested in the space between the sensations. As your attention travels through this space from one sensation to the other, try to find that border again, the border between the 'me' and the 'not me', the border between inside Awareness and outside Awareness, if indeed there is one.

Go back and forth between the two sensations until it is absolutely clear to you, not only at the level of thought, but until you *feel* that these two sensations appear in the same space of Awareness.

Now just allow your attention to wander freely wherever it pleases, encountering thoughts, images, feelings, sensations, sounds. Don't be particularly interested in the content of any experience. Notice that whatever your attention encounters appears in the same field, in the same aware field.

It's a field without divisions within it, without compartments within it. This field is seamless. The field itself is empty of objects, and anything our attention encounters is an object appearing within this seamless field, this seamless, aware field.

*   *   *

Now, instead of directing your attention to the objects that appear within this field, start exploring the field itself. Venture with your attention as far as you can go in this field, and try to find an edge to it. Try to find an edge to the empty, aware field in which your experience appears.

In this way, feel – don't just understand, but feel – that you, this empty, aware field in which all experience appears, has no limit. It has no border. Our attention never leaves it. Our attention never encounters any experience outside this field.

Wherever we do this experiment, be it here, in our homes, if we were on the moon, if we ever land on Mars, we could do this experiment and we would have to admit, 'I never encounter anything outside Awareness.' That is, I, Awareness, never encounters any experience that takes place outside of itself.

I'm not speaking of some extraordinary experience that I am having and that you are not having. I'm just articulating clearly an experience that each of us is having. We may not have noticed it before, but whether we notice it or not, it is still a fact, an undeniable fact of experience. All experience appears in Awareness, and I *am* that Awareness. The body appears in me; I do not appear in it.

Ask yourself the question, 'What is the essential nature of this field?' Don't think about it. Don't work it out with your mind. You are experiencing it, by which I mean you *are* the empty, aware field in which your experience is appearing – that is, in which the mind, the body and the world are appearing. The mind, the body and the world are continuously appearing and disappearing in this field.

What about the field itself? What is its nature? That is, what is *your* nature? What is the nature of 'I'?

Ask yourself the question, 'Does this empty, aware field gain or lose anything by the appearance or disappearance of any particular object?'

Is the field ever stained or hurt or modified when an object appears or disappears? Although this field touches intimately every object that appears within it, each object leaves the field completely untouched.

This field is always in the same pristine condition. It doesn't have to be purified, emptied, silenced or expanded. It is already essentially pure – pure in the sense that it is not mixed with any of the limitations of objects. It is already inherently empty. Its nature is already peace itself. No activity or inactivity of the mind could increase or decrease its inherent peace.

*　　*　　*

Notice that every experience we have – thoughts, images, feelings, sensations, sights, sounds, tastes – all appear and disappear in this empty, aware field. Ask yourself the question, 'When an object appears, where does it come from?' Take a thought, for instance. Thoughts are always appearing and disappearing. What does the thought arise out of? Where does it come from?

Something that appears must come from somewhere. Something that disappears must go somewhere. Don't say, 'I don't know'. You are experiencing the appearance and disappearance of thoughts within yourself, therefore you must be experiencing whatever it is they arise from and disappear into.

Do the thoughts arise from a place outside the empty, aware field? Hopefully, everybody answers 'No' to that question, because we have already discovered that we never find such a place; there is no such place.

Our world culture is founded on the presumption that Consciousness resides somewhere inside the head and that everything else resides outside Consciousness. This is the fundamental presumption upon which our world culture is founded, and yet nobody has ever found this place. It is purely abstract, conceptual thinking that bears no relation to experience whatsoever.

Go back to the thought. Where does it arise? It obviously arises in Awareness. Now ask yourself the question, 'What is there present in the empty field of Awareness prior to the arising of the thought?' There is just the empty field of Awareness. Now ask yourself the question, 'Then what is the thought made of?' It must be made of whatever is present in the empty field prior to its arising.

What is that? Empty Awareness. The thought is made of that. There is nothing in Awareness other than Awareness out of which the arising thought could be made. In other words, when the thought appears, no new substance comes into existence. The thought is a temporary modulation of the eternally existing presence of Awareness. It is a modulation, a temporary modulation of the ever-present substance of Awareness, and as such the thought gives Awareness a temporary name and form. Or we could say, Awareness itself assumes a temporary name and form as it takes the shape of the thought.

It is Awareness itself that begins to vibrate within itself. Every thought is a particular vibration of Awareness, appearing in Awareness, known by Awareness, made of Awareness. But if we ask what it is that is vibrating in the form of the thought, the only stuff there is Awareness or Consciousness itself.

When the thought vanishes, the substance out of which it was made doesn't vanish. It simply ceases vibrating in the form of that thought. Its reality, the reality of the thought, that is, the stuff it was made of, doesn't go anywhere. It simply ceases assuming a particular name and form, and then the next moment it vibrates with a different frequency and a different amplitude. And then Awareness ceases to vibrate at that particular amplitude and frequency and the sound vanishes, but the stuff out of which the sound was made hasn't gone anywhere. It has simply resumed its native state, its original condition.

*   *   *

All experience, if we explore it in this way – and I encourage you to take time to explore all experience in this way – the pleasant experiences, the unpleasant ones, our most loving feelings, our most unloving feelings, our most intelligent thoughts, our most unintelligent thoughts, all experience appears in Awareness, is known by Awareness, and is made of Awareness.

But no experience, no form that Awareness assumes, ever actually divides the field of Awareness into separate objects and selves. It is always one indivisible, borderless field. There are no separately existing objects or selves in this field.

Just like a crowd of ten thousand people seen in a movie don't divide the screen into ten thousand parts – it's always the same indivisible screen – this field, this aware field, is the reality from which all appearances derive their apparent existence. All objects and selves borrow their apparent existence, their apparent individual existence, from this indivisible, empty, aware field.

In religious terms, this field is called God's infinite being. That means, in whom we move and live and have our being. All objects and selves have their being in God's infinite being. Their apparent existence is God's infinite, indivisible being. There is no other substance present in experience.

The existence of individual selves and objects is only real from the illusory point of view of one of those selves. In other words, it is only from the point of view of one of the people in the crowd of ten thousand that there are ten thousand separate people, and from each of those ten thousand points of view there are ten thousand separate objects or others. But from the point of view of the screen, which is the reality of the appearance of ten thousand people, there is just its own seamless, borderless, indivisible self.

The screen never experiences the multiplicity and diversity of objects and others. Infinite Consciousness knows nothing of a multiplicity and diversity of finite experience. The infinite can only know the infinite.

The finite can only know the finite. It is only from the illusory point of view of the finite that there are finite selves and objects. The mind super-imposes its own limit on what it observes, and thinks that that limit is inherent in what it observes. It is not. The limit is in the *way* we see, not *what* we see.

*   *   *

Go to the experience of the body. If we label that experience 'body', then it seems to be something made of matter – solid, dense, limited, located. Remove the label 'body' and replace it with the label 'sensing'. If our eyes are closed, our only experience of the body is sensing. The experience of sensing is made of mind, not matter.

Nothing has changed. The experience remains identical; only the label has changed. But with the change of label, we seem to experience the body in a new way, no longer as something solid, dense, limited, located, made out of matter. Sensing is just mind.

See that it's not sensing *of* the body. The 'of the body' is added by thought. It's just sensing, just mind. See that the mind doesn't appear in something called 'a body', but the body appears in the mind. In fact, the body doesn't appear in the mind; the body *is* mind. All there is to the body is sensing – not sensing of a body, just sensing.

But that's only halfway. See that all there is to sensing is the knowing of it. The only substance present in sensing is knowing, pure experiencing, Consciousness. Just as it was not sensing *of* the body but just sensing, see that it is in fact not knowing *of* sensing but just knowing. All there is to the experience of sensing is knowing. All that is there is Consciousness.

In the first step, we reduce matter to mind. In the second step, we reduce mind to Consciousness. But notice that your experience hasn't changed. Your experience of the so-called body is the same now as it was five min-utes ago. In other words, matter, mind and Consciousness are not three different substances; they are three different ways of experiencing. They are three different names we give to three different perspectives.

In each case, the only stuff present is Consciousness. If we identify Consciousness with the body, experience seems to be made out of stuff called matter. If we identify Consciousness with thoughts and feelings, experience seems to be made out of stuff called mind. And if we identify Consciousness with itself alone, then experience conforms to that understanding and is known and felt to be made of Consciousness alone.

Those are the essential three steps on the spiritual path: the first, I am Awareness; the second, this Awareness that I am is a borderless, indivisible, inherently peaceful field in which all experience appears and with which it is known; and then the third step, everything that appears in Awareness is made of Awareness.

All that remains once these three steps have been clearly seen is to try to lead our lives in a way that is consistent with this feeling-understanding, that is, to think, to feel, to act, to perceive and to relate in a way that is consistent with the implications of this new perspective.

THE WHITE RADIANCE OF ETERNITY

Simply allow experience to be as it is from moment to moment. By 'experience' in this context I mean all thoughts, images, feelings, bodily sensations and perceptions of the world.

See that all these are continuously appearing, changing and disappearing. There is no continuity in objective experience. No thought, feeling, sensation or perception lasts.

Anything that appears and disappears must appear and disappear in something, or on something. It is not possible to have an email without a screen; it's not possible to have the words of a novel without a page; it's not possible to have a cloud without a sky; it's not possible to have a thought, sensation or perception without…without what?

Just as a screen is inherently empty of emails, just as the white page is inherently empty of the words of a novel, just as the sky is inherently empty of clouds, so whatever it is in which thoughts, sensations and perceptions appear is itself inherently empty of thought, sensation and perception.

We cannot turn our attention towards or know objectively whatever it is in which our thoughts, sensations and perceptions appear. We can only know objectively or turn our attention towards thoughts, sensations and perceptions. So don't try to find that in which thoughts, sensations and perceptions appear; it cannot be found or known as an object. That is, it cannot be known by the finite mind.

At the same time, whatever our thoughts, sensations and perceptions appear in is what we call 'myself'. I, myself, am this open emptiness in which all thought, sensation and perception appear. We cannot know that ob-jectively; we can only be that.

When I say, 'we can only be that', it suggests the possibility of being some-thing other than that. It is not possible to be anything other than that. It is possible to believe, imagine or feel that we are something other than that. For instance, we can believe, imagine or feel that we are a mixture of thoughts, feelings and sensations. But even when we believe or feel this, we actually never cease being this open, aware emptiness. Even such beliefs and feelings are appearances in our self, that is, in this open, aware emptiness.

So it is not necessary to work on ourself in order to stop being a finite self, made out of thoughts, feelings and sensations, and instead become a different kind of self, made out of open, empty Awareness. It is just nec-essary to notice that we are already and always only this open, empty Awareness.

Notice that whatever our mind is doing or not doing makes no difference to what we essentially are. What we essentially are remains this open, aware emptiness irrespective of the content of our thoughts, feelings, sen-sations and perceptions. We don't have to make this the case, but rather simply see that it is already the case.

*   *   *

Take three objective experiences: a thought, a sensation of the body – for instance, the tingling at the soles of your feet – and a perception of the world, such as whatever sounds are present. Let your attention wander back and forth between these three objects. Don't be interested in the particular characteristic of each object. Just visit each object lightly, going back and forth with your attention between them.

Ask yourself the question, 'As my attention travels from the thought to the sensation, and from the sensation to the sound, through what medium does it travel?' Does it travel through space, or does it travel through aware emptiness?

Go from the sensation at the soles of your feet to the sensation of your face, and keep going back and forth between these two sensations. In what medium is our attention travelling?

See that the idea of physical space is superimposed on our experience. In our actual experience, attention is travelling through this aware emptiness, or pure Consciousness.

Now take an image, say the image of breakfast this morning. And now take the current thought, irrespective of its content, and allow your attention to wander back and forth between the image and the thought.

Through what medium does our attention travel as it moves back and forth between the image and the thought? Does it travel through something called time, or does it travel through ever-present, aware emptiness?

See that time is never actually experienced. It is superimposed by thought on the empty presence of Awareness.

The finite mind can never know this open, empty, aware Presence, although it is made out of it, just as a character in a movie cannot see the screen out of which it is made. When the finite mind tries to find or know this open, empty, aware Presence, it sees it through the filter of its own limitations and superimposes upon it the concepts of time and space.

In other words, time and space are what pure Consciousness looks like from the perspective of the finite mind. From the perspective of thought, Consciousness appears as time; from the perspective of perception, it appears as space.

The actual medium in which our experience appears is not time and space; it is Consciousness. See clearly that your experience never leaves Consciousness. It never leaves this open, empty, aware Presence.

Just try with your attention to travel to the edge of Consciousness, and if you find an edge, try to step just outside Consciousness. Try to find with your attention something outside Consciousness.

It's not possible. No one has or could ever find such a place. When I say 'no one has or could ever find such a place', I suggest that the one that is exploring Consciousness is something other than Consciousness itself. Consciousness is the knowing element in all experience. Whatever is known is known in Consciousness, by Consciousness, so the phrase 'nobody has or could ever find such a place' should be replaced with 'Consciousness has no knowledge of any experience outside of itself'. For Consciousness, that is, for the one that truly knows experience, all experience takes place within itself, is known by itself and is made of itself.

In our culture we believe that Consciousness is just a little space inside the brain, or that it is generated by the brain. We believe that it is the smallest, most fragile and ephemeral element of our experience. However, this is completely contrary to our actual experience. Consciousness is the largest, most stable, most enduring, most indestructible element of our experience. In fact, it is the only element of experience that cannot be destroyed, removed, altered, stained, harmed or hurt.

So allow yourself to both understand and feel this reversal of perspective. Instead of feeling that Consciousness takes place in the mind, that the mind takes place in the body, and that the body appears in the world, feel in a way that is consistent with your actual experience:

I am the vast, empty, borderless presence of pure Consciousness. It is my being that vibrates within itself and takes the shape of the finite mind, and in the form of the finite mind I appear as thoughts, feelings, sensations and perceptions. That is, I appear as the mind, the body and the world.

* * *

Ask yourself the question, 'What is the essential nature of this aware, open emptiness, other than the fact that it is present and aware?'

Can it be disturbed? See that this aware, open emptiness is like the empty space of a room. Nothing that takes place in the room has any effect on the space itself.

Can this aware, open emptiness be hurt? Can it be modified or changed? Does it appear and disappear? Does it lack anything?

Does it ever go anywhere? Does it ever do anything? Does it ever become sick, or tired, or sorrowful, or old?

Does it ever pass through three states of waking, dreaming and sleeping? Or are the three states of waking, dreaming and sleeping simply modulations of its own ever-present, wide-awake being?

True meditation has nothing to do with a manipulation of thoughts, feelings, sensations or perceptions. It is simply to be knowingly this aware emptiness.

So when this session comes to an end and we open our eyes, don't think and, more importantly, don't feel that our meditation has come to an end.

If we feel that our meditation has come to an end, this feeling betrays the belief that our meditation is a manipulation of objective experience, that it is an activity of the finite mind.

True meditation doesn't start or stop. It has nothing to do with whether our eyes are open or closed, what position we are sitting in, whether there are thoughts or not, whether feelings and sensations are present, or what is taking place in the world.

Simply be knowingly this aware emptiness.

Notice that whatever experience appears, be it a thought, feeling, sensation or perception, it always appears in this empty, aware field. Do we ever experience a thought, feeling, sensation or perception being put in from the outside of this aware field?

In order to answer 'Yes' to that question we would have to experience something outside this aware, empty field. When I say 'we would have to experience', I mean, this aware field itself would have to experience something outside of itself from which the object came. See if you can find that place. That is, see if you, Awareness, can find a place outside of yourself. Can you, Awareness, know or come in contact with anything outside of yourself?

And if Awareness can never find a place outside its own aware emptiness, then everything that appears in experience must appear in and come from this aware emptiness. It's like asking what was present in this room before any objects were placed in it: just empty space.

All there is in this aware emptiness prior to the appearance of thought, feeling, sensation or perception is this aware emptiness itself. Therefore, it is this aware emptiness itself that is the stuff from which everything that appears within it is made. There is nothing in aware emptiness other than aware emptiness out of which any appearance or experience could be made.

That means that all experience – every thought, image, feeling, sensation, perception – is only a modulation, a manifestation of this aware emptiness itself. It means that the fullness of experience is made only of the emptiness of Awareness.

* * *

Take a thought, a simple thought such as the number three. There is no significance to that number.

Just take the thought 'three', and sound that thought in your mind every five seconds or so.

Keep sounding the thought 'three' every five seconds or so, and each time the thought appears, be very sensitive and ask yourself, 'Where is the thought appearing?' And when the thought is present, ask yourself, 'What is it made of?'

The thought 'three' is not nothing; it is something. It has a reality, a substance to it. And just as, if we are experiencing an email, we are by definition experiencing the screen on which it appears and out of which it is made, so if we are experiencing the thought, we are by definition experiencing what it is made of. What is that?

When the thought disappears, what is it that disappears? What happens to the stuff out of which the thought was made? And when the thought appears again, does a new substance come into existence, and if so, where does it come from? What would that substance be? Out of what would its newness be made?

Where would aware Presence find a new substance out of which to make the thought? Prior to the thought, there is nothing in empty Awareness other than its own aware emptiness. Aware emptiness doesn't have a cabinet full of materials out of which to make objective experience. All it has is itself. All it is, is itself.

So when a thought appears, the only substance present there is this aware emptiness. The thought itself is a modulation or vibration of this emptiness. All there is to the fullness of the thought is the emptiness of Awareness.

When the thought appears, no new substance comes into existence, and when it disappears, nothing real disappears. The reality of the thought, the substance out of which it is made, remains the same. The thought is like a colouring of that ever-present substance. It gives that substance a temporary name and form.

* * *

Generate a new sensation by rubbing your fingers together.

Ask yourself the question, 'Where did that sensation come from?' Something that appears must come from somewhere.

See that the sensation appears in this aware, empty field. The sensation did not come from outside this field, and the only substance present in the sensation is the field itself.

Now place your left hand on your left knee. A new sensation appears. Where does it appear? What is it made of? Is there anything there other than the knowing of it? Is there anything there other than this empty, aware field?

Now, leaving your left hand where it is, place your right hand on the chair or floor. A new sensation comes into existence. Where does that sensation appear? Compare this new sensation with the sensation of the left hand on your left knee. Does it appear in the same space or a different space?

When we touch the chair or floor, evidence of a world outside Consciousness seems to come into existence, but is that really true? Does the sensation of the hand on the chair or floor appear outside this empty, aware field?

Take the thought 'three' again, and compare these three experiences: the thought, the sensation of the left hand on your left knee, and the sensation of the right hand on the chair or floor. Do they all appear in the same empty, aware field or a different field?

When our hand touches the chair or floor, we believe that we are touching something that is not ourself. We believe that we are touching something outside of ourself. Go to the sensation of your hand on the chair or floor and ask yourself, 'Is any part of this sensation taking place outside of myself?'

Now take any feeling or emotion that may be present. Where is it appearing? What is it made of? Is there anything there other than aware emptiness?

See that the feeling is just a colouring of this emptiness. It gives this emptiness a temporary name and form.

We believe that thoughts, feelings, objects have existence, or come into existence. The word 'existence' comes from two Latin words, *ex* and *sistere*, meaning to stand out from. Ask yourself the question, 'Does any experience stand out from this field of aware emptiness?' Can we find a thought, feeling, sensation or perception that stands out from, or is removed or separate from, this aware, empty field?

If we think that we do find something that stands out from Awareness, ask yourself, 'Just how far does this thought, feeling, sensation or perception stand out from this aware field?' How much distance is there between an experience and the knowing of it?

The word 'reality' comes from the Latin word *res*, meaning a thing. This etymology betrays our culture's belief that the reality of experience is tested by its thing-ness, its object-ness. But the reality of experience is not made out of things or objects. It is not made out of stuff called matter. There are no independently existing objects. That is, there are no objects that ex-ist, that stand out from, their background of Consciousness and have, as a result, their own independent reality.

Objects, as such, are non-existent. No thing exists or stands out with its own independent reality from Consciousness. Objects do not have existence; they borrow their seeming existence from that which truly is, this aware emptiness, God's infinite being.

When we hear in the traditional non-dual teaching a phrase like 'Nothing ever happens' we may be puzzled, because our experience is so rich, colourful and varied; there is so much happening! So a phrase such as this tends to make us think that the teaching is abstract or philosophical, that it is not related to experience.

On the contrary, it is profoundly and intimately related to experience. It is our conventional way of thinking that is abstract and removed from experience, only we have become so accustomed to it that we mistake it for the reality and intimacy of experience itself. When the teaching states that nothing ever happens, it means no *thing* ever happens, no thing ever comes into existence. No object, self or world ever comes into existence, that is, ever stands out from God's infinite being with its own independent reality.

There is just this empty, aware field, God's infinite being, lending itself to all appearances, seeming to become a thought, feeling, sensation or perception and, as such, appearing as the mind, body and world, but never actually being or becoming anything other than itself.

*   *   *

When a sound appears, ask yourself the question, 'Where is this sound appearing?'

Music playing

See and feel that the sound is just the faintest colouring of this aware field. See that nothing new has come into existence. This empty field is vibrating within itself, taking a new name and form.

Ask yourself the question, 'Is there anything present in the sound other than the experience of hearing?' How far from this empty, aware field does the experience of hearing take place? Is there any substance present in the experience of hearing other than the knowing of it, other than the consciousness of it, the awareness of it?

When the sound gets louder, does it get closer? Or is it always taking place in the same placeless place?

Be very sensitive as the sound disappears. Does the stuff out of which it is made go anywhere? Or does this aware emptiness gradually lose its colouring, lose its name and form?

Music fading out

Where did the fullness of the sound go?

It didn't go anywhere. It was always only a colouring, a modulation of the emptiness of your ever-present self.

And when the fullness of the sound appears again, see that its fullness is only a temporary modulation, a temporary colouring, of your emptiness.

Music playing, then ending

Where does the reality of the sound go as it vanishes? It is only you, I, this empty, aware field, that ceases vibrating within itself at a certain frequency and thus ceases appearing in the form of the sound. But the stuff that is vibrating, that is, you, I, this empty, aware field, doesn't go anywhere. It doesn't go out of existence. It never came into existence in the first place.

Nothing exists. No thing exists. No thing has its own independent being. That which is never ceases to be. That which is not never comes into existence.

The Sufis say the same thing in their own way: *La ilaha illallah*, 'There is no God but God.' There is no thing, there is no object, self or world, that has its own being, its own existence. The only being there is, is God's infinite being. There is no God but God. There is no being other than God's infinite being. All seeming objects and selves borrow their apparent existence from the only one that truly is: God's infinite being.

The primary purpose of that which seems to come into existence is to announce and celebrate that which eternally is.

*   *   *

Allow your eyes to open, but only a millimetre. This empty, aware field just assumes a new colouring, just a pale watercolour wash over its transparency.

Does the experience of seeing take place outside the empty, aware field, or is it simply a temporary colouring of that field?

The experience of seeing gives this empty field a new name and form. In Sanskrit, name and form are *nama* and *rupa*. There is a beautiful equation in Sanskrit which is the essential equation of all experience: *Nama rupa sat chit ananda*. All names and forms are simply temporary modulations of this ever-present, self-aware, inherently peaceful being.

Allow your eyes to open two millimetres. The colours get a little stronger, but experience never leaves this empty, self-aware field. No thing comes into existence.

As the poet Shelley said, 'Life, like a dome of many-coloured glass, stains the white radiance of eternity.' Of course, he didn't really mean 'stains', in the sense of sully or dirty. He was referring to a stained-glass window which colours the sun's transparent light. So he really meant, 'Life, like a dome of many-coloured glass, *colours* the white radiance of eternity.' Nothing stains the white radiance of eternity.

Now allow your eyes to fully open. Look around, but look in a kind of disinterested way, totally relaxed, just seeing without seeing any particular thing.

The experience of seeing is a colouring of this empty, self-aware field. It is a colouring of the white radiance of eternity, a colouring of God's infinite being.

The first thing that any objective experience tells us, before it tells us anything about a mind, a body or a world, is about God's infinite being.

All experience announces God's infinite being. All experience shines with God's infinite being. As the Sufis say, 'There is only God's face.'

Life, like a dome of many-coloured glass, *shines* with the white radiance of eternity.

This is what the poet John Keats meant when he said, 'Beauty is truth, truth beauty. That is all ye know on earth, and all ye need to know.'

THE GREAT EMPTINESS

Be knowingly the open, empty presence of Awareness in which all experience appears, with which it is known and out of which it is made.

Allow your eyes to open, and just let your attention rest on whatever objects appear. Understand that when we open our eyes, all that changes is that seeing appears.

Slowly trace the experience of seeing back to its source. So we withdraw the focus of our attention from the seen object and, as it were, travel backwards to the source of seeing, to the place from which seeing proceeds.

Notice that as we approach the source of seeing we don't arrive at something called 'a body'. We cannot see or even experience the body as it is normally conceived. All that is known of the body is a flow of sensations and a few perceptions.

What do we really find at the source of seeing? Where does the experience of seeing come from? Don't think about this. If we are experiencing seeing, we must be experiencing that from which it proceeds.

All we find is an openness, an emptiness there. It is from this emptiness that seeing proceeds. It is not proceeding from a body. If we trace the experience of seeing back to something that we previously considered to be our eyes, we don't find any object there called 'eyes'. We just find an openness, an emptiness there, the absence of an object.

It is this emptiness that allows the objects that we see to come into existence. If this openness were full of anything other than emptiness, there would be no room for the fullness of the object within it.

This emptiness is not only an absence of objects; it is also an absence of space. Space is part of the seen. Seeing does not take place in space. Seeing proceeds from and takes place in an openness, an emptiness that has no finite qualities. As such, it is infinite. It is infinity itself.

Right here, at the heart of our experience, the placeless place from which seeing proceeds, is itself infinity. This placeless place is not in space; space proceeds out of it. In fact, space doesn't proceed out of it; space appears within it.

It is as if there were a doorway in the back of the mind. Seeing proceeds out of that doorway towards the object. If we follow the experience of seeing in the other direction, backwards, as it were, towards its source, we go through that doorway into infinity.

That is the heart of our self – the dimensionless, objectless, placeless place from which seeing proceeds. Where we previously thought we would find a body, we now find this dimensionless emptiness.

*　*　*

Allow a thought or a series of thoughts to arise. The content of the thoughts doesn't matter. To begin with, with your attention, follow the thoughts towards the objects to which they refer.

Now, instead of following a thought in the direction of the object to which it refers, trace the thought back in the other direction. Follow the thought in the other direction, towards the place from which it proceeds.

Notice that when we arrive at the place from which thought proceeds, we don't find something called 'a mind' or 'a brain'. We arrive at a great openness, an emptiness, out of which the thought proceeds and into which it returns when it comes to an end.

It is as if there were a second doorway in the back of the mind, out of which thought proceeds and through which it returns. Behind that doorway is a vast emptiness. That emptiness is not in time. Time comes into apparent existence with the appearance of thought. That vast emptiness is itself ever-present, or eternal.

These two doorways – the one out of which perception proceeds, and the other from which thought proceeds – open onto the same dimensionless, empty space. This emptiness is called infinity in reference to perception. It is called eternity in reference to thought.

Eternity and infinity are the two names for the same emptiness, from which all thought and perception proceed and to which they return when they come to an end. This emptiness doesn't appear in time or space. Time and space, plus the thoughts and objects that they contain, proceed out of it and dissolve back into it.

*   *   *

Allow your eyes to close, and let the current sensation come to your attention. Know nothing about the sensation other than the current, direct experience of it. Without reference to thought or memory we have no idea that the current sensation is something called 'a body' sitting on something called 'a chair' or lying on something called 'a floor'. It is just an amorphous, borderless, tingling vibration with no well-defined shape, no edge, no age, no gender, no nationality, no weight.

Ask yourself the question, 'What is this vibration appearing in?' Thought would like to say, 'a body', but this sensation or vibration doesn't appear in a body. Our only experience of the body is itself simply this vibration. When we trace back the vibration in order to find its location, we don't find that it is located in something called 'a solid body'. What do we find?

We don't find anything, that is, we don't find any *thing*. The place at which this vibration is appearing is completely empty, open, transparent. Even those words seem to give it subtle qualities that it doesn't really have. It is an absence that is not only the absence of an object, but even the absence of all these qualifying adjectives – open, empty, transparent. We simply cannot go there with thought. And yet, at the same time, it is our experience that this vibration is appearing in this unnameable, indescribable, utterly intimate emptiness.

This emptiness is sometimes described in the spiritual literature as a spacelike presence, and that is a valid concept in the early stages of this exploration. But go beyond even that spacelike quality. Ask yourself the question, 'How large is this vibration?'

Can we measure its size? Is it a centimetre wide? A metre wide? Ten metres wide? We cannot say. Why can we not say? Because this vibration doesn't have a dimension. It is not appearing in space; it is appearing in dimensionless emptiness.

In fact, we cannot even say that it's appearing *in* this dimensionless emptiness, because that immediately gives it a spatial quality. Don't try to think about this. It is not possible to think about something that has no dimensions. That is why Shantananda Saraswati said, 'Real thinkers don't think.' That is, if we really want to think about the nature of reality, or the reality of our experience, thinking will bring itself naturally, effortlessly to an end.

See that this vibration completely fills the emptiness. There is no part of the emptiness where the vibration is not present, and the emptiness pervades and saturates the vibration.

Don't try and think about this. We are exploring experience in a way that is beyond the reach of thought. It can only be experienced; it cannot be thought about.

When viewed from the outside, this vibration that we once called the body seems to be a temporary, limited object appearing in time and space. When viewed from the inside, the only substance present in this vibration is eternal, infinite emptiness.

Allow the vibration and the emptiness to mix so completely with one another that we cannot tell them apart.

If a feeling of boredom, frustration or irritation arises, see that all that is happening is that this emptiness is taking the form of a thought and a feeling and, as such, entering the doorway back into the mind and going outwards towards an object.

As thought proceeds through the doorway it comes out of eternity, into time. All that the thought is trying to do in time is to avoid the emptiness of eternity. In fact, the reason that thought is seeking an object is in order to merge with that object and cease being thought. In other words, thought is seeking to bring itself to an end. It is seeking its own eternity, but it is seeking it in the wrong direction; it is seeking it in objects.

Thought is proceeding from the feeling of boredom, frustration or irritation, trying to relieve the discomfort of these feelings in objective experience. It is seeking eternity in time.

Gently turn the seeking thought around. Trace it back through the doorway at the back of the mind and return it to its source in eternity.

*   *   *

Let your eyes open again, and allow the appearance of space and the objects within it to come into existence, but don't let the appearance persuade you to believe or feel that this dimensionless Presence has left itself, or come in contact with anything other than itself.

We don't have to reject the appearance of space and objects, but rather feel that they are saturated, permeated with this emptiness. They are a modulation of this emptiness itself.

If we find that the appearance of space and objects is too persuasive or overwhelming, we simply trace back the experience of seeing to its source. See that the body we once imagined ourself to be is not in the picture. If we trace seeing back to its source there is just a vast emptiness at its origin. We fall through the eyes into this emptiness.

It's like the wardrobe in *The Lion, the Witch and the Wardrobe*, which is a magical portal into an enchanted forest. We trace back the experience of seeing to what we thought was something called 'my eyes' or 'my head', but at the moment we touch that place we fall into a new dimension. We fall into eternity.

*   *   *

Now just allow your attention to range freely over the entire realm of experience: thoughts, feelings, sensations, sights, sounds. See that we never leave this emptiness. This emptiness never leaves itself.

All experience is saturated in this dimensionless Presence. Nothing can harm it, nothing can destroy it, nothing can alter it, and yet it is completely vulnerable, it is completely open, it is completely without resistance.

This dimensionless emptiness modulates itself in the form of the fullness of all experience.

In this approach, meditation is not an activity. It is not a manipulation of our experience. It is not something we start doing, or stop doing, with the mind. It is, first, to recognise the nature of experience, and then simply to abide as that in the midst of all experience. In this approach there is no distinction between meditation and life.

Now we just go about our day as normal, but don't be persuaded by appearances to believe or feel that something called meditation has come to an end. True meditation doesn't start and it doesn't end. Only this dimensionless emptiness assumes new names and forms.

From the outside, experience is ever-changing; from the inside, never-changing.

THE MAGNIFICENCE OF GOD'S INFINITE BEING

Allow a thought or series of thoughts to come to your attention, and notice that each thought is about some kind of object or objective experience.

We might be thinking of a friend, we might be thinking of the weather, we might be thinking of our family, we might be thinking of what we're going to do this afternoon. Notice that whatever we are thinking about is some kind of object, and the object about which we are thinking is not itself the thought. The thought is about the object, about something other than itself.

If we think of the rain, the rain is an object to which the thought refers, but the rain to which the thought refers is not itself a thought.

Now, ask yourself the question, 'Does a thought ever come in contact with the object about which it is thinking?' Can a thought about rain ever touch the experience of rain? Does the thought of a friend ever touch or come in contact with the friend about which it thinks?

See in this way that the thought, in fact, never comes in contact with its object. There is no connection between the thought and its object, and therefore it cannot legitimately be said to be a thought *about* something or someone. The thought never comes in contact with the someone or something. There is no connection there. All the thought comes in contact with is the presence of Awareness in which it appears.

Allow, in this way, the thought to be liberated from its apparent connection to an object. See that it is just free-floating in the empty space of Awareness. It's like an island in the ocean: all it is in contact with is the water of Awareness.

Now take a feeling. Notice, to begin with, that the feeling is always about someone or something; it is a feeling *of* something. Ask yourself the question, 'Does the feeling ever actually come in contact with the object or person about which it feels?' Does the actual feeling itself ever touch or come in contact with the person on whose behalf the feeling is taking place? See in this way that there is no connection between the feeling and the object or person.

It is not a feeling *of* someone or something; it is just a feeling. The feeling itself never has an object. The only thing, if we can call it a thing, that the feeling ever comes in contact with is the empty space of Awareness in which it appears.

The feeling, which is inside of us, never comes in contact with the person, who seems to be outside of us. They never meet, and therefore we cannot legitimately say it is a feeling about a person. This is more difficult to see in relation to our feelings because of the emotional charge, the connection with the person on whose behalf the feeling seems to arise. But be courageous: see that the feeling is just a feeling. It is not a feeling of or about someone or something.

If you feel reluctant to let go of the 'of someone' or 'of something', don't worry; we will find them again later. Let go of the object or person to whom the feeling seems to refer. Just experience the feeling itself, free-floating, surrounded on all sides by the open, empty space of Awareness. The feeling never comes in contact with anything other than Awareness.

See what happens to the feeling, see how it evolves, when it is just experienced in this way, free-floating without any connection to anyone or anything, simply suspended in the empty space of Awareness.

See how the feeling evolves when it is liberated from the object or person. The feeling ceases to have a direction – a direction towards the object or person. It is not going anywhere. It is just suspended in the empty, space-like presence of Awareness. Let the feeling soak in that Presence.

*   *   *

Place your hand on the chair or floor. A new sensation comes to your attention. Thought tells us that it is a sensation *of* something. Go to the actual experience of the sensation. Without reference to thought or memory, would you know that the sensation is a sensation of something?

In the experience, is there one thing called 'sensation' and another thing called 'chair' or 'floor'? If that were the case the sensation would be made of two separate elements: one, the sensation, and two, the chair or floor. There would be a line down the middle of the sensation that divided these two elements. Is that the case? Or is the sensation one seamless, indivisible experience in which both the so-called hand and the so-called chair or floor are experienced as one?

See in this way that it is not a sensation *of* something. The 'of something' is added by thought, but as we have already seen, the thought about the sensation never comes in contact with the sensation itself, so thought can tell us nothing about sensation. They do not meet. The sensation itself is not a sensation of something; it is just sensation. And that sensation is simply appearing, suspended weightlessly, in the open, empty, spacelike presence of Awareness, the same Presence in which our thoughts and feelings are appearing.

Notice that we are not manipulating our experience; we have done nothing to change our experience. All we are doing is experiencing it as it is, and allowing the experience itself to be liberated from the concepts that thought has superimposed upon it. The experience itself hasn't changed; its nature is being revealed.

Don't do anything to the sensation itself. Just see that it is already floating in, appearing in, the empty space of Awareness. Awareness is the only thing, if we can call it a thing, that the sensation is in contact with. When you move your hand and the sensation disappears, it simply merges into Awareness. When you put your hand back and a new sensation appears, it simply appears in Awareness.

*　　*　　*

Now take the hand of the person sitting next to you. Take some time to allow any awkwardness to subside. Take some time to ascertain in your actual experience that all you know is a sensation. Without reference to thought or memory, you have no idea that it is a sensation of someone else, or that you are touching someone else.

Take some time for the sensation to be liberated from any superimposed beliefs and, more importantly, superimposed feelings which may arise, such as the feeling of awkwardness. See that those feelings themselves are not in contact with anything other than the presence of Awareness. Those feeling are not feelings *about* a sensation. They are just feelings, not feelings about anything; let them go. Come back to the sensation.

Is the sensation composed of two elements, one element called 'me' and another element called 'not me', one part that is appearing in myself and another part that is not appearing in myself? Or is the entire sensation one seamless, intimate, indivisible whole – not a sensation *of* someone or something but simply a sensation, appearing in the open, empty, spacelike presence of Awareness?

I am not denying that there is a feeling of connection, communion, but what is the reality, the actual reality of this feeling of connection? What is the sensation connected to? Can a sensation be connected to a thought? Does a sensation touch a thought or an image? No, the only thing, if it can be called a thing, that the sensation touches, the only thing that the sensation is intimate with, is Awareness.

You can let go of each other's hands, unless of course you want to keep holding hands!

As the sensation subsides and vanishes, it reveals the Presence in which it was appearing. For those of us in intimate relationships, it's very interesting to explore this in the experience of sexual intimacy. Two sensations never touch one another. All we ever experience is our own sensations. We cannot experience somebody else's sensations.

The intimacy in sexual union is not the merging of two sensations, not the merging of two bodies. Two bodies, two objects, never touch or come in contact with one another. The merging is the merging of the sensation in Awareness. The bliss is the inherent bliss of Awareness making itself known as the sensation dissolves into it.

When two people experience this together, what they are enjoying is not the union of two people. A person is a mixture of thoughts, feelings, sensations and perceptions. No thought, feeling, sensation or perception ever comes in contact with or touches another thought, feeling, sensation or perception.

The bliss of union is not the merging of two bodies; it is the dissolution of two sensations into the same space of Awareness. Our union, the feeling of union, is the sameness of the space of Awareness which our sensations share. Two objects can never be unified. The feeling of union is only the *prior* unity of Awareness revealing itself as our sensations dissolve into it.

Anyone who has experienced sexual intimacy without this feeling of union knows how boring it is. What we love in this intimacy is the bliss of our true nature. What we taste in this intimacy is only the bliss of our true nature. What is revealed in this intimacy is not a meeting of objects. It is the prior bliss of our true nature.

When an object such as a sensation merges into the Awareness from which it has arisen, Awareness briefly shines as it is. And then, when the sensation arises again, Awareness is colouring itself in the form of that experience. Then, as it ceases to colour itself in the form of the sensation, it briefly shines again. That self-shining is the experience of happiness.

*   *   *

Allow your eyes to open. See that the perception of the world comes to your attention, or at least that's what thought says. Are you sure that it's a perception of the world, rather than simply a perception? See if you can find a difference now between your current experience of the perception and your perception of the world. Is there anything to our experience of the world other than perception?

All there is to our experience of the world is perception. How do we know it is the perception *of* something? Do we ever find the something, the world, independent of perception? Try now to experience the world independent of your perception.

It's impossible. Nobody has ever or could ever experience a world independent of perception. So how do we know that we are experiencing a world? We don't. All we can be certain of is that there is perception. We have no idea that the perception is a perception of something. The 'of something' is added by thought.

The belief that our perceptions are perceptions *of something* is the fundamental presumption upon which our entire world culture is founded.

It is the presumption of materialism. Not only do we believe that we are having a perception of the world, although nobody has or could ever come in contact with the world. We go a step further in our abstract, convoluted thinking and believe that the world creates perception. We believe that the world was here first and that the ability to perceive is a by-product of that world.

Has anybody here ever experienced that world, the world outside perception? Notice again that we are not manipulating our experience; we are not doing anything to it, trying to change it, to improve it, to meditate it away. We are just exploring it as it is, and as we explore it we allow our experience to be divested of the layers of belief and feeling that thought has superimposed upon it, allowing the so-called world to reveal its nature to us, allowing its nature to be revealed.

So, allow your experience of perception to be liberated from the belief that it is a perception of something. It is just perception.

Ask yourself, 'What is my perception appearing in?' It is not appearing in space. Our only knowledge of space is a perception. That perception is not appearing in space; space is appearing in perception. So what is that perception appearing in? Perception appears and disappears, and anything that appears and disappears must appear and disappear in something or on something. What is that?

The current perception is appearing in the open, empty, spacelike, but in fact dimensionless presence of Awareness. Yes, that means that what appears as three-dimensional space appears in and is made of something which itself has no dimensions. That should blow your mind.

Remember, we're not talking abstract philosophy here. All we are doing is exploring our experience – not some extraordinary experience that I have and none of you have, but the experience that each of us is having, the ordinary experience that each of us is experiencing all the time.

We think that our experience of the world is illuminated by the sun. Of course, relatively speaking, everything we see is a modulation of the sun's light, but that experience is *known*. What is it that knows that experience? What is it that illuminates the light of the sun? What is it that renders the sun's light, and all the colours and shapes we see, knowable? Consciousness.

Think now what Jesus meant when he said, 'I am the light of the world.' The 'I' that he was referring to is the 'I' that each of us knows ourself to be. His 'I' was our 'I'. The 'I' in him is the 'I' in us, or the 'I' of us. It is our shared Consciousness, the only Consciousness there is, that shines in each of our minds as the knowledge 'I', or 'I am', or the feeling of being, that illuminates experience, that contains and illuminates experience.

All the objects that we see in the world are, relatively speaking, reflections of the sun's light. If the sun's light were to disappear now, there would be no experience of objects. In just the same way, all that we are really experiencing in reality are reflections of the light of Consciousness. It is the one single light of Consciousness that is being refracted as the multiplicity and diversity of our experience. Just as all the objects in the world seem to be refractions of the sun's light, all that is being experienced are the modulations of Consciousness, and it is Consciousness that is experiencing itself in the form of those modulations.

Everybody feels that there is one world, in spite of the fact that that single world appears to them as a multiplicity and diversity of objects. If our only knowledge of the world is a multiplicity and diversity of objects, how come we all feel that it is one world? How come we all feel it is the same world that we are experiencing, even though each of us only knows the world through our private perceptions?

Our perceptions are never shared. None of you can see what I am seeing, and none of us can see what each of you are seeing. Our perceptions are private, and yet we feel deeply that the world we experience is shared. There is some truth in that belief, but what each of our private perceptions share is not the world – it is Consciousness.

Each of our perceptions, each of our private perceptions, is appearing in the same shared Consciousness. It is only when we overlook the presence of our shared Consciousness that thought projects the sameness of Consciousness onto the world and believes, as a result, that it is the same world that we are experiencing. No, it is the same Consciousness that we are experiencing.

So there is some truth in our intuition that there is one world, that we share the world. The intuition of oneness is correct, but thought wrongly ascribes oneness to the world. It is Consciousness that is one, and the world is experienced as a unity insofar as it partakes of that oneness. It is the oneness of Consciousness that is shining as the singularity of the world.

Before our perceptions tell us anything about a world, they tell us about the nature of that from which they arise, that out of which they are made and into which they merge. Our perceptions shine with the light of Awareness. They announce the light of Awareness. They celebrate the light of Awareness.

*   *   *

Allow your eyes to close again. Allow the current sensation to come to your attention. Take some time to allow the sensation to liberate itself from any belief that it is a sensation of a body. It is not a sensation of anything; it is just a sensation. Take some time to not simply understand that intellectually, but to feel that.

Ask yourself the question, 'Does the sensation have a clearly defined shape? Does the sensation have a size?' How big is a sensation? Don't refer to thought or memory; refer to the raw experience itself.

Does the sensation have a gender? Does it have a weight? Go to the apparent experience of weight. Our only knowledge of weight is a sensation. Are we sure it is a sensation of weight? Or is it just a sensation, floating weightlessly in the dimensionless presence of Awareness?

Notice again that we are not manipulating our experience. We are simply allowing experience to be divested of superimposed concepts and feelings. Divested of its size, its shape, its gender, its age, its weight, what is the sensation? What is really there? Can we actually find a discrete object called 'a sensation'? Can we take a sensation, as it were, out of Awareness and place it on a table? Is a sensation something in its own right? Does it have its own independent existence? Is there such a thing, such an object, as a sensation?

See that there is no object there, no discrete object with its own clearly defined shape, size, border or weight. It is not really a sensation; it is a process of sensing. The sensation is not like a fish in the ocean with a clearly defined outline; it is more like a current in the ocean. We can take a fish out of the ocean. Relatively speaking, it has its own independent existence. Can we take a current out of the ocean? There is no such thing as a current as opposed to the ocean. There is just a modulation of the ocean. The current is a temporary name and form of the ever-present, formless ocean.

The only substance present in sensing is knowing, Consciousness. The experience of sensing gives this nameless, formless knowing a temporary name and form. But no discrete object ever comes into existence – existence, remember, from *ex sistere*, 'to stand out from'. The current never stands out from the ocean. No thing ever comes into existence. Nothing exists.

All that truly is in experience is Consciousness. And whilst Consciousness modulates itself in the form of sensing, in the form of all experiencing, it never ceases to be itself, never becomes anything other than itself, never becomes an object that exists. No thing ever stands out from Consciousness.

Apparent objects borrow their existence from the only one that truly is, Consciousness itself, or God's infinite being, God's infinite, self-aware being.

Reality is neither something nor nothing. There are simply no things present in reality to which reality can be contrasted or defined.

*   *   *

Allow the current thought to come to your attention. Do we ever actually experience a discrete object called 'a thought'? Take the thought, 'What a beautiful, rainy day it is today.' When the 'What' sounds in your mind, where is the 'a beautiful, rainy day it is today'? And when the 'a' sounds in your mind, where is the 'What' and where is the 'beautiful, rainy day it is today'? They are non-existent. When the 'beautiful' sounds in your mind, where is the 'What a' and the 'rainy day it is today'? They are not present. Even in the word 'beautiful', when the 'beau-' appears, where is the '-tiful'? And when the '-tiful' appears, where is the 'beau-'?

We never experience a discrete object called 'a thought', or even 'a word'. There is no thing there. There is a process of thinking, not an entity or object called a thought. It is not the thought *of* a beautiful day; it is just a thought. It is not the thinking of a thought; it is just thinking.

But what is thinking made of? Is there anything to thinking other than the knowing of it? Try now to find any substance present in the experience of thinking other than the knowing of it. All that is there is knowing – not even the knowing *of* it. Knowing never has an object.

It is thinking alone that divides knowing into a knower and the known, into a subject and an object, into mind and matter, into self and other. The only actual substance present in thinking is knowing.

What you are hearing now is not the sound of a voice; it is just a sound. It is not the hearing of a sound; it is just hearing. It is not the knowing of hearing; it is just knowing.

What we are seeing now is not a sight of the world; it is just sight, or perception. It's not the seeing of a sight; it is just seeing. It is not the knowing of seeing; it is just knowing.

Reduce all your experience into Consciousness. This is another way of saying, see clearly that the only substance present in experience is Consciousness. Allow experience to be merged in Consciousness.

For the infant and the animal, Consciousness is merged in experience. For the one who has recognised the nature of reality, experience is merged in Consciousness. For the animal and the infant there is only experience. For the one who has recognised the nature of reality there is only Consciousness. In both these cases there is only one thing. For the child, it is experience; for the sage, it is Consciousness.

For this reason these two perspectives have some similarities and are often confused in superficial, New Age approaches to non-duality. What we are speaking about here is not going back to an infantile, pre-verbal way of seeing our experience. We are not returning to the pre-egoic state of infancy; we are evolving into the post-egoic realisation. Both perspectives share some qualities in terms of innocence and spontaneity, but there is a difference between them. For the infant and the animal, Consciousness is merged in experience, and for the sage experience is merged in Consciousness.

In between these two stages there is egoic life, in which the seamlessness of pure experiencing that the child knows is divided into an experiencer and an experienced. In the post-egoic recognition this distinction is again collapsed.

This is what they mean in Zen when they say that first the rivers are rivers and the mountains are mountains. That's the child's experience: there are only rivers and only mountains; there is only experience. Then the rivers are no longer rivers and the mountains are no longer mountains. That is the halfway stage, enlightenment, the recognition of the presence, the primacy and the nature of Awareness. And then the distinction between Awareness and its objects is collapsed, and the rivers are rivers again and the mountains are mountains again.

As Ramana Maharshi stated it, 'The world is unreal. Only Consciousness is real. Consciousness is the world.'

As it is expressed in the Christian tradition, 'I and my Father are one': What I, Consciousness, am and what the ultimate reality of the universe is are the same.

As the Sufis say, 'Whosoever knows their Self knows their Lord': Whosoever knows their self knows the ultimate reality of the universe.

As the poet John Milton said, 'Come ye winds who from four quarters blow, and sing His praise': Everything announces the presence of God's infinite being. Everything sings praise to God's infinite being.

Think of the magnificence of the universe, and then think that that magnificence is only a partial revelation of the magnificence of that out of which it emerges, and of which it is made. Is it even possible to contemplate that magnificence?

The mind falls silent in the face of that magnificence. As the painter Chatin Sarachi once said to my mother, 'If God exists, how do you dare even mention his name?'

THE TRANSPARENT SUBSTANCE OF THE BODY

I want to say a little more in general about this approach to the yoga. In order to discover whether our essential nature of pure Awareness is limited or not, we begin with a rational approach, exploring and exposing all the beliefs that suggest that Awareness is limited, discovering one by one that they have no actual basis in our experience.

This is a process that Atmananda Krishna Menon called 'higher reasoning'. By higher reasoning, in contrast to what is normally considered to be reasoning, Krishna Menon meant a line of reasoning that comes from direct experience rather than from beliefs. We could call it 'experiential reasoning' to distinguish it from mere abstract philosophy.

This deep investigation of the belief in being a temporary, finite self, living in and as the body, has a counterpart in the exploration of our actual experience of the body. Just as beliefs become fixed in the mind, so ways of feeling, moving and relating become enshrined in the body. These habits, in which the belief in being a separate self is substantiated in our feelings at the level of the body, are laid down over many years and become the deeper core of the separate self or ego.

We don't just believe, 'I am a separate, temporary, located self'; we feel it. The top layer of these feelings, most of which reside in the chest area, are fairly easy to identify: 'I feel hurt', 'I feel upset', 'I feel lonely', 'I feel unloved', 'I feel unworthy', 'I feel guilty'. These feelings are not quite as clearly delineated as our thoughts, but nevertheless they are clear. They have a name and a shape and a location.

But there are other layers of feeling, below these more obvious feelings, which are less clearly defined, a kind of nameless, formless sense of lack or fear or resistance. We feel them, but we don't feel them as cleanly and as clearly as we do the feelings of sadness, loss, sorrow, and so on.

As we go deeper into our feelings, deeper down into the well of feelings, the feelings become less clearly defined and less clearly located. So the explorations or contemplations that we do in these yoga sessions are to the body what higher reasoning is to the mind. Instead of engaging lines of reasoning, we engage lines of movement or feeling-imagination, such as expanding the body in all directions into empty space, filling the whole space of the room. Just as higher reasoning liberates our self from self-imposed beliefs, this Tantric Yoga of Sensation and Perception liberates the body and the world from self-imposed feelings.

Just as, in our conversations, we consider the possibility that Awareness is unlimited and ever-present, and, as a result of this consideration, expose and confront all the beliefs that seem to oppose it, so in this yoga we explore visualisations and postures that expose the separate-self feeling in the body, flushing it out of its hiding places and offering it to the open, empty space of Awareness.

In this offering, in which the body is expanded beyond its customary limits, resistances and habits that are consistent with the belief in a solid, dense, located body, and which have been laid down over many years, are exposed and revealed.

However, just as the purpose of our conversations is not to arrive at new certainties, conclusions or assertions, but rather to expose and dissolve old beliefs, so once this yoga has done its job of exposing and revealing these habits and tensions, it too should be abandoned, and the body is left in a new configuration, without concepts or formulas.

This Tantric Yoga of Sensation and Perception exposes old patterns and habits of feeling in the body. But we shouldn't think that the exercises we do here are supposed to be maintained throughout the rest of the day. We simply undertake them in the laboratory of our yoga sessions and allow their effect to percolate into our daily experience.

In fact, the benefits of this yoga are not something that the mind is usually party to. Don't expect something extraordinary to happen during our yoga contemplations. Something unusual may happen, but that is not the purpose. The benefits of this approach to yoga are usually felt after the yoga session, in the coming days or weeks, and may not even be registered by the mind.

The dissolution of the feeling of the separate 'me' is not something that the mind is party to. The mind doesn't notice when the separate self vacates the body. It's like having a headache in the morning and deciding to go out for a walk. We go out for a walk, and two or three hours later we return and suddenly notice that our headache has gone. We didn't notice when our headache disappeared. We just offered our body to the favourable conditions, in this case fresh air, and the fresh air took care of the headache without the mind knowing how or when the dissolution took place. We just notice when we get home that we had completely forgotten about our headache.

It's the same here. The separate self leaves the body without the mind knowing how or when. All that is necessary in these meditations is to participate with an open mind, an open heart and an open body. We let the open, empty space of Awareness take care of the residues of separation in the body. Don't try to take care of them with the mind. Don't even expect the mind to notice the process. At best, the mind may notice later on that old feelings, contractions and reactivity have simply ceased appearing in our experience. They are no longer controlling and affecting our relationships, activities, movements and feelings.

*   *   *

So, first of all let us explore what we really mean by the experience of the body.

I suggest to begin with that we do this with our eyes closed. The only reason for closing our eyes is that it removes visual perception. In other words, it removes our experience of the world and enables us to really focus on the body.

First of all, think about your body, or think a series of thoughts about your body. See clearly that those thoughts are thoughts *about* your body, but they are not your body itself. So put those thoughts on one side. We won't be referring to them again. We don't have to get rid of them; we just put them on one side.

Now take the image of your body, the image you might see when your eyes are open, in a photograph or looking in a mirror. Again, that is not the body; it is an image of the body. Put that image on one side. We won't be referring to it again.

Now go to what remains of your experience of the body. That is what we call a sensation: a tingling, amorphous, vibrating mass of sensation. That is our current, direct experience of the body.

What is it that is going to explore the body? Only that which knows it can explore it. So establish that you are the knowing with which this sensation is known. You are just pure knowing. All you can do is know, or experience. You cannot think; you cannot speak. You're just made of pure knowing, pure registering, pure sensitivity.

Imagine that you are a newborn infant that can only experience, but has absolutely no idea what it is experiencing. You are this newborn knowing. You have nothing to refer to apart from this current experience.

In order to express what you find – what you, this pure knowing, finds – you need a means of expression. So, on your explorations, take thought with you.

It's like a politician travelling in a foreign country, taking an interpreter with him. When the politician gets interviewed the interpreter doesn't answer the questions; he just interprets what his employer says. Thought is like that. You, pure knowing, relay what you find to thought, and thought formulates it. But thought only formulates what comes directly from pure knowing.

So we now embark on this tour of the body to discover what it truly is. Feel and visualise, to begin with, that you are a little particle of knowing, and with thought by your side you dive into the sensation. You start swimming around in it with the sole purpose of knowing, experiencing what it truly is.

Swim to the sensation that thought calls 'my head' or 'my face'. Immediately drop the label or image of face or head, and as this particle of knowing, swim around inside this sensation. Ask yourself, 'How dense is it in there?' Do you ever come across an obstruction as you swim? Does anything resist you, as you, this particle of knowing, swim around exploring the sensation from the inside?

Thought can formulate the answer, but it is you who do the exploring. Don't let thought answer for you.

Notice that as you swim you come across some areas that seem denser than others. Swim into these denser areas. How dense are they? Is there any obstruction to this free movement of pure knowing?

Swim back and forth from the dense areas to the less dense areas, taking little samples or specimens as you go. Now, compare the two different substances that you find: a sample that comes from the dense area and a sample that comes from the less dense area. What is the essential difference, if there is one, between these two different substances?

Now flow from the less dense areas into the empty space around the sensation. Take a sample of it, swim back into the sensation and compare the two: the sample from the space around the sensation and the sample from the substance inside the sensation. Don't think about it; you are just made of pure sensitivity, pure knowing.

Keep swimming back and forth between the sensation and the space around it, sampling the two. How would thought formulate the difference between these two samples?

As you flow back and forth, as you swim back and forth from the inside of the sensation to the space outside it, pay particular attention to the threshold where you cross from one to the other. Can you find that edge? Don't say either 'yes' or 'no' too quickly. Explore this edge, this transition, from the sensation to the space all around the sensation. Don't just explore the border in one place. Swim in and out of the sensation all over its surface, looking for the border.

See in your experience that we never find that edge. It's like walking from England into Wales, expecting to cross the border between the two countries. We never find it. The border is on the map, not on the ground. The border is in our thoughts and images but not in our experience.

* * *

Now, swim back into the sensation and swim downwards to include the neck, chest and belly area. All we are doing is knowing our experience, tasting experience itself, intimately, to find out what is really there.

Be very sensitive to the areas that seem more dense. Flow back and forth between the dense areas and the less dense areas, trying to find the line that divides them, if there is one.

If you were to take a sample of this substance, pure sensation, and ask thought to describe it, try to find the words that best describe the stuff that this sensation is made of.

Continue swimming around. Go into the pelvic area and the legs. As we swim around there, something interesting happens. We come across something that thought labels a 'chair' or a 'floor'. Tell your interpreter to keep quiet, and proceed very cautiously. Go up to the edge, the place where the body, the sensation, stops and the chair or the floor starts.

This time, instead of swimming from the sensation to the space around it, swim back and forth from the sensation to the chair or floor, looking for the frontier, looking for these two substances, one, called sensation, and two, called chair or floor. Can you find these two substances?

When you flow from one to another, do you cross a threshold, a line that separates one from the other? Or is it just the same stuff wherever you go?

Now we have three samples to compare: sensation, space, and chair or floor. Swim around in and out of the sensation, from sensation to space, from space back inside the sensation, from the sensation to the chair or floor. You are pure sensitivity, pure knowing, pure experiencing. Do you find three different substances?

Go to the experience that thought labels 'weight'. See that that experience is itself just a sensation: 'weight' is a sensation plus an interpretation. Leave thought's interpretation on one side. Go to the raw sensation and swim around in it. How much does a sensation weigh?

Swim around between the space, the sensation and the chair or floor. Thought tells us that one is empty and transparent, one is semi-solid, and one is dense, solid, inert. It should be easy to swim around in the space, less easy to swim around in the sensation, and impossible to swim around in the chair or floor. Is that your experience?

Do you, as a particle of pure knowing, ever come across any obstruction to your flowing, anything that resists you? Or is it the same stuff everywhere?

See that the borders, the descriptions, the differences exist only on the map, not on the ground – only in thought, not in experience.

*   *   *

As you swim around as this particle of pure knowing, or pure sensitivity, you begin to expand. Very gradually, this tiny particle of knowing grows into the size of a walnut…you keep swimming around…then into the size of an orange…then a melon…then a pumpkin. You are changing from a particle of knowing into a field of knowing.

You keep swimming around, and as you swim around you are beginning to expand into the sensation, through the sensation, through the chair or the floor, into the space all around. This field of knowing seeps out in all directions, all over the sensation – in front, behind, above, below – permeating and colonising whatever it finds in its path.

This field of knowing expands in all directions, beyond the sensation, and fills the room, tasting, sampling, experiencing, knowing everything it comes in contact with.

Now you are no longer swimming around. You are too large to swim, so you've become stationary, motionless, just a field of pure knowing. You begin to feel that the sensation is very slowly swimming around in you.

As the body moves with every breath, very slowly, the sensation undulates. It is flowing in you; you are no longer flowing in it.

As the sensation gently undulates and flows in you, you keep sampling what it is made of. You are the knowing field in which this sensation is flowing. You take two samples again: one, a sample of yourself, pure knowing, and two, a sample of the sensation.

Do you find two different substances there? Can you find an edge where the sensation stops and the knowing field in which it flows starts? Is there any part of the field of knowing that is not totally pervaded by yourself? Do you stop at the edge of the sensation?

No. We have been swimming around in this sensation all morning. We cannot find any substance in the sensation that is other than this knowing field. The sensation is like a current in the ocean, made only of water. The sensation is like a current or an eddy flowing gently in this knowing field, made only of this knowing field.

You are not made out of a body. The body is made out of you. It is one thing to know this; it's another thing to feel this.

*   *   *

Allow the sensation to expand in all directions into the knowing field in which it appears, with which it is known, with which it is saturated and out of which it is made.

As this current, this vibration, expands in all directions into the knowing field, so the knowing field continues to expand and colonise the entirety of your experience. It flows through the walls and finds no obstruction there. It flows out into empty space in all directions.

It comes across something that thought calls 'sound'. It touches it, but finds only the knowing of it there, finds only itself, a vibration of a slightly different frequency than the vibration called 'my body', but nevertheless a vibration of the same substance: pure knowing, pure sensitivity. The sound is just another current in the ocean, made only of water.

For this pure knowing there is no such thing as 'near' or 'far', no such thing as 'me', 'you' or 'it'.

Now, the last step: we remove the spacelike quality from this knowing. We see that the idea of a vast, borderless space is a subtle superimposition. In this moment we have no experience of space. It is not a knowing *space*; it is pure, dimensionless knowing, and everything this knowing comes in contact with is made out of itself, *is* itself.

All experience is this dimensionless knowing, vibrating within itself, modulating itself in the forms of thinking, feeling, sensing and perceiving but never being, becoming or knowing anything other than itself. This absence of anything other than itself is the experience of love or beauty.

Now don't do anything. Just let experience be as it is.

PURE KNOWING IS OUTRAGEOUSLY PROMISCUOUS

Be knowingly the luminous, open, empty field of pure knowing in which thinking, sensing and perceiving arise, with which they are known and out of which they are made.

Don't pay lip service to this idea. See that in our experience, each of these three – thinking, or the mind; sensing, or the body; and perceiving, or the world – is made only of the knowing of it. Knowing is the common denominator of thinking, sensing and perceiving – the mind, the body and the world.

Pure knowing is Shiva. Thinking, sensing and perceiving are Shakti. Shakti emerges out of Shiva but never leaves Shiva. Shakti dances in Shiva. Thinking, sensing and perceiving emerge, not *out of* pure knowing but *within* pure knowing, and dance in knowing.

See that all we know of a mind, body or world are thinking, sensing and perceiving. Thinking, sensing and perceiving appear in pure knowing, are made only of knowing and are known by knowing. This knowing only ever knows itself. Shiva gives birth to Shakti within itself and knows Shakti as itself.

It is only a thought that abstracts from this seamless intimacy, from this marriage of Shiva and Shakti, a multiplicity and diversity of objects and selves called the mind, the body and the world. With that idea alone, which thought superimposes on the intimacy of our experience, Shiva and Shakti divorce.

The separate self is the offspring of this divorce, and it spends the rest of its life trying to reunite with its source, to heal the pain of the divorce, the pain of separation.

In our conversations together it is like being in the classroom, where we explore all these ideas, but in these yoga meditation sessions we come out of the classroom and we enter the laboratory. We explore the ideas that we have been discussing, not just intellectually but in a visceral, experiential way. It is a way of bringing our intellectual understanding into the felt, lived experience of the body and the world.

The laboratory is a transitional phase between the classroom and the field, the field being everyday life in the world. So these experiential contemplations that we do in the yoga meditation sessions are the prelude to taking our understanding not just into our feelings in the body, but into our activities, perceptions and relationships in the world.

*   *   *

Now, instead of understanding and feeling yourself to be a field of pure knowing, in which thinking, sensing and perceiving arise, understand and feel yourself to be a particle of pure knowing.

As this particle, you dive into the experience of thinking, sensing and perceiving. You taste it, as a particle of pure knowing, from the inside, not as an outside observer. You are not the witnessing presence of Awareness in the background of experience. You are a particle of pure knowing in the foreground, at the heart of all experience.

Start with thinking. Allow a series of thoughts to appear. It doesn't matter what the thoughts are; all that is required is to sample the substance out of which thought is made from the inside. We taste the thought from the inside.

The content of the thought is irrelevant. We have no interest whatsoever in what the thought is saying; all we're interested in is the stuff out of which the thought is made. Our thoughts may be peaceful or agitated, true or false, kind or unkind, profound or trivial; it makes no difference. In each case, each of these thoughts is made only of thinking. We are interested in the substance, the reality, the stuff out of which thinking is made.

Now, having sampled the stuff that thinking is made of, you, as a particle of pure knowing, flow from the experience of thinking into the experience of sensing, being very sensitive to any border you find between thinking and sensing. One of our missions in the lab is to see if we can find a place where thinking comes to an end and sensing begins, where one object called 'the mind' ends and another called 'the body' begins.

This particle of pure knowing travels backwards and forwards, to begin with, between thinking and sensing, seeing if it ever crosses a threshold, if it ever meets with any resistance as it enters the experience of sensing. Does this pure knowing have the experience of entering something a little bit more solid than thinking, a little bit more dense? Or does it just glide seamlessly, effortlessly, from thinking to sensing?

Then the particle swims around within the entire volume of sensing, taking samples. Sometimes the experience of sensing may be bland, sometimes it may be a little more intense, sometimes it may be what thought calls painful, but just as we have no interest in the content of our thoughts, so we have no interest in the outer form of the sensation, the label that thought gives it. Pleasant, neutral, painful – it's irrelevant. All we are interested in is the substance, the nature, the reality, the stuff out of which sensing is made.

So we travel around the entire volume of sensing, taking samples. What do I actually find there? What substance is present there? Do I ever come across a substance that is different from myself, different from pure knowing? Do I ever encounter any kind of resistance as I enter something called a 'pleasant' sensation or an 'unpleasant' sensation, or even a 'painful' sensation?

Is it a little bit more difficult to flow as a particle of knowing into the painful sensation than it was to swim around in the pleasant sensation? Does the painful sensation offer some resistance to my knowing, or is it totally open, totally without resistance, totally transparent?

See clearly that I, the particle of pure knowing, glide effortlessly, seamlessly into the middle of this so-called painful or unpleasant sensation.

Ask yourself the question, 'What substance do I find there?' I, the particle of pure knowing, swim around, comparing samples as I go, occasionally revisiting the experience of thinking, collecting samples, comparing them. Do I ever find any other substance than knowing, all equally empty, all equally transparent? Wherever I go I find only myself.

Now I begin to venture out of the experience of sensing into the experience of hearing, being very careful to explore the boundary, if there is one, between these two territories. Go very slowly as you approach the border. Do you leave one substance called 'sensing' and enter another called 'hearing'?

Do you leave one object called 'a body' and enter another called 'the world'? What do these labels, 'body' and 'world', mean to you from the inside of experience, from the heart of experience? They are meaningless. We have not encountered an object called a mind, a body or a world. We have only encountered our self, pure knowing.

Chainsaw sound

Ask yourself the question, 'Is the experience of hearing slightly denser than the experience of sensing? Is it made out of a different substance?'

Children's voices

Explore the entire volume of hearing. We are not interested in the labels that thought adds to the experience called 'chainsaw', 'Rupert's voice', 'children talking'. These are as irrelevant as the content of our thoughts and the quality of our sensations. We're only interested in the substance, the reality, the nature of hearing.

As the sound gets louder, thought says that it is getting closer, and as it gets quieter, thought says that it is moving farther away, but what do you say – you, the particle of pure knowing? Are you getting closer to hearing at one moment and farther away from it at another? Or are you totally married to hearing at every moment?

See clearly that you know no distance, no space, no otherness, between yourself and experience.

Swim back and forth freely between these three realms, which are, in fact, only three realms from the point of view of thought. They are one realm to you: not thinking, sensing and hearing, but rather thinkingsensinghearing. They are only conceived as three separate substances when the knowing out of which they are made is overlooked, when their common denominator is forgotten. At that moment, three substances come into apparent existence. They never actually come into existence – they never leave pure knowing, or become anything other than pure knowing – but only seem to from the point of view of thought.

*   *   *

Now allow the eyes to open, but only a couple of millimetres, not so far that a recognisable world comes into view, just a millimetre or two. All that is seen is abstract colour. Thought doesn't yet know what it is. You are still just a particle of pure knowing.

We swim around inside the experience of seeing, but we go very slowly. We're familiar with swimming around in thinkingsensinghearing. Now we, this particle of pure knowing, enter this new volume called 'seeing', and we pay very particular attention to the border, if there is one, between thinkingsensinghearing and seeing.

Do we leave one object and enter another? Do we ever have the experience of leaving a mind and entering a world, leaving a world and going back inside a body? Or is the transition between thinkingsensinghearing and seeing completely seamless?

We flow effortlessly from one to the other. In fact, it's not 'from one to the other'; there aren't two different spaces there. It's all one space, one volume. All we come in contact with is the experience of seeing. We sample each colour and each shape.

Now allow the eyes to open halfway. We taste the experience of seeing from the inside; we're not observing it from the outside. We take a sample from each colour and ask ourself, is there anything there in that particular modulation of seeing that is made out of anything other than the knowing of it?

Now we allow our eyes to open fully, but we have no interest in the content of what we see. It is the substance of what we see or know that is of interest – its nature, its reality. We are still a particle of pure knowing, swimming around inside what we now call thinkingsensinghearingseeing.

Don't let thought tell you a story about a mind, a body or a world. See that Shiva and Shakti are at all moments happily married. It is only one of their offspring, a single thought, an adolescent thirteen-year-old boy, who causes conflict between them and seems to separate them.

Now, instead of keeping our head focused in one direction, we start looking around. We have no interest in the content of what we see. We are interested only in its substance, its reality.

Experience is always one seamless, intimate whole. Even to call it think-ingsensinghearingseeing is not quite right. That is only right from the point of view of mind. From the point of view of knowing – which at this stage is still from the point of view of this particle of knowing, right at the heart of experience – there are not four separate substances here, thinking, sensing, hearing and seeing. There is just one substance, know-ing, and it is knowing that knows this knowing.

Keep looking around with this disinterested gaze. Now the particle of pure knowing begins to expand until it becomes a field of knowing. The field of knowing assumes the form of the field of thinkingsensinghearingseeing. So we first visualise, and then feel, that the particle of knowing expands into this amorphous volume called thinkingsensinghearingseeing.

We are no longer a located particle. We are a field. And the field of thinkingsensinghearingseeing is identical to the field of knowing. It is, we could say, a colouring, like a watercolour wash, on the field of knowing.

Someone sent me a quote from Henry James this morning where he says, 'Everything about Florence seems to be coloured with a mild violet, like diluted wine.' Pure knowing is bathed in this colourful wash called think-ingsensinghearingseeing. In fact, it is this knowing that vibrates within itself at a particular frequency and assumes the colours, the forms, of thinkingsensinghearingseeing.

Thinkingsensinghearingseeing is just another name for pure knowing. Shiva has become Shakti. Shakti has become Shiva. In fact, they haven't become one another, because they were always identical to one another, always married, always in love. Only thought seemed to separate them.

Shakti is an emanation of Shiva, an expression of their union, an expres-sion of their love. This is what William Blake meant when he said, 'Eter-nity is in love with the productions of time.'

Pure knowing is outrageously promiscuous. He sleeps with everyone he comes in contact with. He makes love with everyone and everything, in-timately and indiscriminately. He's not choosey. If she shows up as Shakti, that's fine. If she shows up as Kali, that's fine.

*　　*　　*

Now we add another layer of experience: movement. We are slowly transitioning from the lab to the field. We first go from the classroom to the lab, and then from the lab into the field of everyday life.

The body comes to the kneeling position. We are kneeling on all fours, on our hands and knees. Just adapt these suggestions to whatever is comfortable for you. We have no particular interest in physical postures. We don't even know things called 'physical postures'; we take only one posture in this yoga. It's called Shiva Asana, to stand as pure knowing, the posture of pure knowing. That is the only posture we take in this yoga.

Our back rises slowly, like an ocean swelling…only knowing, knowing only knowing…and now collapses…and rises again, rhythmically, like an undulating wave, the back arching and collapsing in your own time.

Add breathing into the mix. Lengthen and deepen the breath, but know only knowing. Be the knowing that knows only itself. See clearly for yourself that the substance called 'breath' is no more transparent than the substance called 'hands on floor'. There is no density or solidity there. There is only knowing, knowing only knowing.

Long, slow, deep, rhythmical breathing, in harmony with the movement of the waves. Know only knowing. Be only knowing. The wave rises up and the hips swell up towards the ceiling.

Come all the way up until your legs and arms are straight in Downward-Facing Dog posture, and whilst remaining on the same spot, rise alternately on your toes as if you were going for a walk along a country lane. Nothing changes. Sample every experience you encounter. Have no interest in the content of experience, only its substance. Don't let thought tell you a story about easy or difficult, pleasant or unpleasant.

The left foot comes forwards to the hands, the right knee rests on the ground, the arms flow up to the ceiling. Know only knowing. Be only knowing. For those who want to, raise your right knee off the ground. Don't let thought tell you a story about unpleasant or difficult.

Come back. The hands flow down. And now the same on the other side. Know only knowing. Feel that the intensity of sensing increases, but the stuff out of which it is made doesn't change.

Come down. The legs and arms straighten again, and we slowly walk the feet up to the hands. We hold the backs of our ankles gently, without grasping them. We visualise and feel that the upper body is like the crest of a wave breaking on the shore. Visualise, first of all, the way in which a wave reaches its peak and begins to break and flow onto the shore, and having visualised that, we feel the quality of that movement and we infuse our experience of the body with that feeling.

Just let your hands fall loosely. The upper body flows like a wave onto the ground. Close your eyes if you can keep your balance. Because there are no limits to pure knowing, this sensation can flow well beyond the physical limits of the body, so the wave flows onto the ground and spreads out. This is all done with our feeling-visualisation. The wave spreads out onto the ground and begins to permeate the ground, seeping into it, and because the ground is made of pure sensing, it offers no resistance to the wave.

Take a step back with the right leg. Both hands are now hanging either side of the left leg, resting very lightly on the floor. Visualise and feel that your hands are resting on the tummies of two newborn babies. We don't want to hurt the babies.

Then we allow the wave to fold over the left leg. Don't let thought tell you a story about unpleasant or painful. The field of knowing knows no such thing. It knows only itself, which is neither pleasant nor unpleasant.

The right leg comes back and we do the same on the other side. Adapt the posture to your body. The wave flows over the right leg.

We come back, bringing the legs together, and then, very slowly, we begin to grow into the standing position. But before we do so, we visualise a plant growing. How much effort does it take for a plant to grow? Having visualised the plant growing, we then visualise the body coming to the standing position, but we don't yet move the body. Stay with the upper part of the body folded over the legs like a falling wave, and just with your feeling-imagination, the body comes to the standing position. It is a flow of emptiness moving in emptiness, knowing knowing only knowing.

This time we take the so-called physical body with us, but we infuse the quality of the previous visualisation into our movement. We first visualise the effortless quality of a plant growing. We feel emptiness moving in emptiness. And then the body slowly grows upwards into the standing position in a way that is consistent with this feeling: emptiness moving in emptiness, knowing knowing only knowing.

*   *   *

Now we take a pause on our walk along the lane. We admire the view. The view here is called thinkingsensinghearingseeingbreathing: knowing modulating itself in the form of thinkingsensinghearingseeingbreathing, but never knowing, being or becoming anything other than itself.

Still in the standing position, the right knee floats up to the horizontal. It flows up to the chest and we wrap our hands around it. We hug the knee to the chest. Don't let thought tell you a story about pleasant or un-pleasant, easy or difficult. It's all the same stuff.

The knee comes down. It pours back down and touches the ground. It pours into the ground. Visualise the wave called 'leg' resting temporarily on the ground and then flowing into it, pouring six feet into the ground. Visu-alise and feel the right leg like a column of water pouring into the earth.

Now the left knee floats up. We gently hug the knee to the chest. Know only knowing. Have no interest in a posture, a movement, a position, a body or a practice. If thought tells you something about unpleasant or painful, don't do what thought wants you to do, which is to avoid it. Go towards it. Go right to the heart of what thought labels 'unpleasant'. See if you can find anything there other than knowing, other than your self.

The left leg comes down. The right foot comes across the left thigh and you allow the arms to grow up towards the ceiling. Again, first visualise the way in which a plant grows effortlessly, and then, with that feeling, the arms grow effortlessly up towards the ceiling. The plant grows up, the water flows down. The plant is touching the ceiling, the water is flowing into the ground.

Come back. The same movement on the other side, the right leg straight like a waterfall pouring into the ground, the left leg folded across the right thigh, and the arms growing effortlessly towards the ceiling like a plant: the tree pose.

Come down. We pause again on our walk along the lane. We admire the view. The view is thinkingsensinghearingseeingbreathing. And now we add the last layer of experience: relationship, conversation.

So, everybody start talking. Just to begin with, start talking very quietly to yourself, whatever your thoughts are. Just talk quietly out loud. Have no interest in the content of your talking. Know only knowing.

Thinkingsensinghearingseeingbreathingtalking, all one seamless, intimate substance, made only of knowing.

Now start walking on the spot, but continue talking. We go back to our walk along the lane and we continue our talking. We know only knowing: knowing knowing only itself.

And now, staying only as this knowing, knowing only this knowing, instead of walking on the spot we start walking around the room. We roll up our yoga mats, we talk with our friends, we go and make ourself a cup of tea. We continue our normal, everyday life.

We are moving from the laboratory into the field, out into the world of everyday experience. Our yoga session hasn't come to an end; true yoga, true meditation, never starts or comes to an end. There is no real distinction between meditation, yoga, everyday life, experience and our self. The stuff out of which experience is made, its reality, never begins and never ends.

THE TRUE BODY OF ETERNAL, INFINITE CONSCIOUSNESS

So, welcome back to the laboratory of experience.

We have a concept and a feeling of a body that is solid and continuous. As a solid object it is believed and felt to exist in space. As a continuous object it is believed and felt to last in time. Space and time are thus considered to be the medium in which the solid, lasting body exists.

In fact, a solid, lasting body is a concept that is superimposed on our experience. In just the same way that we can never see the same river twice, so we can never experience the same body twice.

The actual experience of the body is a continuously changing flow of sensation. The feeling of a solid, lasting object called 'a body' is just a mirage. It seems to be there, but when we go up to it and try to touch it, we don't find something that is solid, made of matter, existing in space and continuous in time.

Having said that, there is something substantial and continuous in our experience of the so-called body. Where does this apparent substantiality and continuity of the body come from?

Our essential nature, as we have discovered, is simply being aware. These two elements, being and knowing, constitute our essential nature, or they are, rather, two aspects – not two separate parts, but two aspects – of our undivided nature.

At the level of a human being, the being aspect or the existence aspect – *sat* in Sanskrit – takes the form of sense perception and appears as an object, a substantial object in space. The knowing aspect in a human being takes the form of thought or mind and appears as continuity in time.

So the apparent substantiality and continuity of the body are not properties of a physical object called a body. The apparent substantiality and continuity of the body are derived from pure Awareness, from the infinite being and the eternal knowing that are inherent in what we essentially are.

This being aware at the level of the human being, at the level of human experience, appears as objects that exist in space and last in time. That is, the body borrows its apparent substantiality and continuity from our infinite, eternal nature. The apparent substantiality and solidity of the body is in fact our infinite nature, infinite being, filtered through sense perception. The apparent continuity of the body is the eternal nature of pure Consciousness filtered through mind.

Thus the body, and indeed the world in which the body appears, is like a snapshot at the level of human experience of the infinite, eternal nature of pure Consciousness. There is no real, solid, continuous object there, just like there is no single object called a river that is always the same. The name 'river' is just a placeholder. Likewise, the label 'body' is just a placeholder for something that is not solid in space or lasting in time.

The body and its world are infinite, eternal Consciousness, taking shape through sense perception and thought, or filtered through sense perception and thought, appearing as a substantial, lasting object called a body.

If we overlook our essential nature of being aware, we attribute the qualities that properly belong to Awareness to the body. We think that the body is substantial and continuous; it is not. It is Awareness that is infinite and eternal. The stuff the body is made of is infinite, eternal Consciousness. That is all that is there.

That is the theory, and it doesn't matter if you don't understand the theory. In time it will become clear. To some of us, what has just been said will seem heady, abstract and intellectual. To others, it will be seen as a simple, clear description of our experience. So don't struggle with what has just been said. What is far more important is to feel the body in a way that is consistent with reality.

*   *   *

In this lab of experience, we go very deeply into our actual experience of the body, progressing very slowly and sensitively, divesting the body of all the limitations that thought and feeling have superimposed upon it, leaving the actual experience of the body, the true body, revealed: the true body of infinite, eternal Consciousness.

The first thing we do is drop the label 'body', which is a very inaccurate label for our actual experience, and we try to find another label that comes a little closer. If our eyes are closed the so-called body is just experienced as sensation – tingling, shapeless, borderless, genderless, ageless, vibrating sensation – suspended not in a physical space, because with our eyes closed we have no knowledge of physical space, but rather suspended in a knowing space, or a field of pure knowing.

Notice that as soon as we label the body in this way, something very strange happens: we experience it in this way. If we label our experience 'solid, dense body', we experience a solid, dense body. If label our experience 'quivering, vibrating, borderless sensation', we experience a quivering, vibrating, borderless sensation. See how happy your experience is to be relieved of this first layer of superimposed belief. See how the experience of the body itself conforms so willingly to our new understanding.

Remember, you are a newborn infant. You have no past to refer to. You are just a field of pure experiencing, pure sensitivity, and this strange creature, this quivering, vibrating sensation, has just appeared in your midst. You have no idea what it is. It is just a vibration – nameless, shapeless, genderless, ageless, borderless vibration – suspended weightlessly in this empty field of pure sensitivity, pure knowing, a field of pure experiencing.

This quivering vibration is just suspended weightlessly in this open, empty field of pure experiencing, always gently undulating, never the same thing from moment to moment.

Notice that this quivering vibration is pervaded by the field of experiencing in which it appears. The black dots don't really interrupt the white paper. The white paper is not just around the outside of the dots, but each dot itself is surrounded by a field of white paper. This tingling vibration doesn't just appear in this field of knowing or experiencing; it is permeated by it.

Now, visualise and feel that this vibration begins to gently expand in all directions into the empty field of pure experiencing. And just a word about what I mean by 'visualise and feel'. We first visualise it, but then we actually feel it. It doesn't mean imagine it; it means actually do it: expand this vibration very gently in all directions.

In fact, let's break it down. Start with the front of this vibration. Visualise and feel that this vibration begins very slowly to expand into the space in front, into the knowing space. It's a feeling-visualisation.

Now visualise and feel the vibration expanding backwards into the knowing space. Notice that it may be a little more difficult to expand the sensation backwards, because our sense faculties are in the front of the face. We are familiar with the space in front of us. The space behind us is always unknown; it is always dark. We can never see that space, so it feels unfamiliar or dark, and for that reason it is a little more difficult to feel the expansion of this vibration into the space behind.

The feeling of difficulty is actually a resistance, and this resistance is being exposed by our attempt to expand the sensation backwards. So don't feel that the difficulty is a failure; on the contrary, it is working. It is revealing the resistance, the concept we have superimposed upon our experience: this space behind is somehow dark or unknown. How can something made of knowing be unknown?

Now visualise and feel the vibration expanding into the space above.

Now into the space below. Notice again that there may be some resistance to expanding this vibration into the space below. Ask yourself why. Your actual experience is that this vibration is just suspended weightlessly in this empty field of pure knowing. If there is some resistance to expanding this vibration into the space below, it is because you are subtly superimposing the concept of a solid, dense floor underneath you. In other words, you are referring to memory, to thought, not to your actual experience.

The experience of a solid, dense floor or chair is itself just a quivering vibration. There is nothing solid or dense there. This vibration is suspended in this vast, empty space, floating weightlessly in it.

It takes some time, usually several attempts, to feel that it is equally easy to expand this vibration in all directions. If you encounter a resistance, particularly in the space behind or underneath, don't see it as a failure, something to be struggled with. On the contrary, it is the revelation of a resistance of which we were previously unaware. It is coming up to the surface of our attention. Just go very slowly and meet that resistance with your experience.

All you know is the knowing of your experience. How is it possible for something to be unknown? The unknown cannot be. Nobody has ever experienced the unknown.

*   *   *

Now stop compartmentalising this knowing field and just continue to allow this vibration to expand in all directions. Notice that as the vibration expands it begins to thin out, like a dense cloud gradually expanding into the sky and thinning out as it does so.

It's as if the dots on your white page are spreading out all over the page, and as they spread out the drawing becomes less and less dense. More and more white paper appears around each dot.

As this vibration evaporates in all directions into this knowing field, it thins out, revealing more and more of the knowing field within the vibration. The vibration is becoming thinner, less dense.

If you notice the tendency to get lost in thinking, again, that is just a subtle resistance. What is actually happening is that the body is wanting to shrink back into the old way of being felt as something solid, dense and continuous. To avoid this dissolution into emptiness, we are getting lost in thought, we are being distracted by a thought, thereby allowing the body to resist this return to its true nature. The body just wants to maintain the old, familiar patterns.

So if you notice yourself lost in thought, just gently bring yourself back. Don't feel that to be lost in thought is a failure of this meditation; on the contrary, it is the exposure of a resistance. Having noticed it, just come gently back to this expansion and try again.

This 'trying again' seems at first to be an effort we are making. In fact, it is not a new effort, but rather the revelation of an old effort of which we were previously unaware, that is, the old effort to feel the body as something solid, dense, limited. So it is not a new effort that we are making, but rather the relaxation of an old effort of which we were previously unaware.

In other words, this is not something we are doing; it is the cessation of something we were previously doing. But if it doesn't feel like that, if it feels like it is something you are doing, that's fine. Just do it. Make the effort, this gentle, loving effort to feel this vibration expanding slowly, seeping, like a drop of ink on a piece of blotting paper, seeping slowly out in all directions into this empty field of knowing.

Notice that there may be some areas of this vibration that yield very willingly to this expansion, but there may be other areas that are more dense, more contracted, that seem more solid, that are, as a result, less willing to yield to this expansion. If that is the case, go to these areas, take them one by one, and very lovingly, gently, slowly encourage them, entice them, persuade them to gently let go and expand into this space. The space is friendly. It is supporting. It is allowing.

Notice that as this vibration spreads out and begins to fill the entire field of pure knowing or experiencing, it becomes less and less easy to distinguish the two – one, the vibration, two, the field of experiencing.

The cloud has evaporated and dissipated into the space all around and just hangs like a thin mist, filling the entire space. It becomes less and less easy to distinguish the mist from the space. The mist is like the thinnest watercolour wash over the space. So this vibration is like a thin wash over the empty field of experiencing. It becomes less and less easy to distinguish two substances there.

Go back and forth between the vibration and the field of experiencing. Can you find two objects to go back and forth between?

See, which means *feel*, in your experience, that there is just one substance there: this empty, luminous field of pure experiencing, vibrating within itself. This vibration gives it a temporary name and form, but it never ceases to be what it eternally is: one eternal, infinite substance, that is, one ever-present substance that in itself has no limits, that vibrates within itself, thereby assuming an apparent limit that has a name and a form, but never actually being, becoming or knowing anything other than itself.

This absence of otherness or object-ness or two-ness is the experience that for a human being is expressed as love, peace, beauty and fulfilment. In Sanskrit it's called *ananda*. For those of you who are familiar with Sanskrit terminology, this meditation is a feeling-understanding of the exquisite Sanskrit formulation of the nature of reality: *Nama rupa sat chit ananda*.

Sat, being or existence, appears for the human being as the perception of objects in space. *Chit*, Consciousness or pure knowing, takes the shape of knowledge or thought in time. Thought gives experience its name;

perception gives experience its form. Thus it is the infinite, eternal substance of our own being, pure Consciousness, that, vibrating within itself, assumes a name and a form and appears as such in time and space.

When name and form, time and space dissolve back into their dimensionless origin, the experience of love or peace or beauty is revealed.

DISSOLVING THE BODY IN EMPTY OPENNESS

Be knowingly the openness in which all experience appears. It is on account of our emptiness that the fullness of experience is possible.

Allow the sensation of the head to appear in this empty openness. Immediately drop the label 'head'. Just experience this sensation or vibration floating weightlessly in open emptiness. Take some time to allow the image and the memory of the head to fade, leaving only the raw sensation itself.

The image and memory of a head are the past; they are an abstraction. They are not the actual experience of the current sensation. They are an image and a thought superimposed on the current sensation. Stay only with the sensation, the vibration itself.

In order to speak of it, I have to name it. But as soon as you have heard the name, drop the name. It is only meant to take us to the direct experience.

Allow this quivering vibration to float weightlessly in this empty openness.

Feel that the face is a dense mass of quivering vibration, and that the back of the head, unless we have a headache, is completely empty. In fact, it is so empty that we don't have a 'back of the head'. The back of the head is completely open to the space behind. There is no boundary there, separating a head from the space.

Feel that the face is like a rich tapestry of sensation, suspended weightlessly in this empty space. Visualise and feel the empty space in front of the sensation of the face, and allow the sensation to very gently expand into that space, just a couple of inches. It's all done with our feeling-imagination.

We can first visualise the sensation expanding into the space. That visualisation creates a kind of pathway, and then with our feeling-imagination we follow that pathway. We take that pathway and allow the sensation itself, the feeling of the sensation, to expand along that pathway a couple of inches into the space in front.

If you feel some resistance, don't feel that this is a sign that you are failing at this contemplation. On the contrary, it means the contemplation is working perfectly. The resistance is the exposure of an old, previously unnoticed habit of feeling the head as a solid, dense, located object.

The face is one of the favourite locations of the apparently separate self in the body: 'I, the seer', 'I, the hearer', 'I, the taster', 'I, the smeller', 'I, the thinker'. So the separate self, the imaginary separate self, has a vested interest in keeping the experience of the head in general, and the face in particular, exactly as it is, because in doing so it can maintain its illusory identity.

When we make the attempt to expand this sensation of the face beyond its customary limits into the space in front, the separate self that lives in this dense mass of sensation first is exposed and then begins to rebel: 'I don't want to do this, because in doing this I am going to be expanded beyond my customary limits', or 'I can't do this, because in doing this I'm going to be discovered, exposed'.

It's one thing to think that the separate self doesn't exist; it's quite another to feel it. So, if we feel some resistance, we just pause. The resistance itself is some kind of sensation or contraction. Allow that sensation to gently expand into the space in front.

If we find ourself getting lost in thought, then we see that these pathways of thought are simply avenues of escape for the separate self. They simply prevent the deeper aspect of the separate self, which is a feeling in the body, from being first exposed and then dissolved. So if we find that our attention has gone on a little excursion of thinking, we gently bring our attention back to the sensation of the face, and make the effort again to expand the sensation into the space in front, just a couple of inches.

And now six inches into the space in front. Don't feel, 'I can't do this'. If we are doing our best to do it, then we are doing it perfectly.

Twelve inches in front.

And then we just keep allowing the sensation to seep out into the empty space. Go very slowly. Decades of conditioning are being confronted by this simple contemplation. Decades of conditioning that 'I am a solid, dense, located entity' are being exposed and challenged by this simple contemplation and, without our necessarily realising it, are being dissolved by this contemplation.

*   *   *

Now, leaving the vibration expanded in the space in front, visualise the space behind the face. Don't superimpose the image or memory of a head. It's all empty space. First visualise and then feel that the vibration begins to seep backwards into the space. We first visualise it, and this visualisation creates a kind of pathway into which the feeling of the vibration subsequently flows.

There is sometimes more resistance to expanding the vibration into the space behind than into the front, because the space behind seems to be less well known than the space in front. This feeling that the space behind is less well known is just a memory, an idea superimposed from the past. See that there is, in fact, no difference whatsoever between the space behind the face and the space in front. Both are equally familiar, both equally intimate.

Feel that the vibration of the face expands all the way into the space behind until it touches the wall behind us. First visualise the wall, then visualise the space between the vibration and the wall. First visualise the sensation expanding slowly through the space until it meets the wall. This visualisation creates a kind of pathway for the sensation to follow. Then we drop the visualisation and feel that the sensation or vibration seeps backwards into that space. As it seeps backwards it expands, and as it expands its density thins out.

Feel the sensation on the left-hand side of the face. Be very sensitive. You are made of pure sensitivity. Feel the temperature of the air on your left cheek. Drop the labels 'air' and 'cheek'. We know nothing of air or cheek, just a subtle vibration suspended weightlessly in empty openness.

Feel the subtlety and richness of the tapestry all over the left-hand side of the face. First visualise and then feel the space to the left of this sensation. Visualise the sensation flowing into the space. This visualisation creates a pathway, and then we allow the feeling of the sensation to gradually expand into and seep along this pathway into the space.

If there are thoughts or feelings, 'I can't do this' or 'I don't want to do this', that's very good. These are simply signs that the apparently separate self is being exposed and flushed out of one of its favourite hiding places.

Feel that the sensation expands all the way up to the wall on the left-hand side. The sensation caresses the wall.

Now allow the sensation of the right-hand side of the face to come to your attention. Feel the temperature of the air on your right cheek. Drop the labels; it's just a vibration. Visualise the space to the right, and then feel the vibration expanding and seeping into that space.

Visualise the empty openness below the sensation of the face. Visualise the quality of liquid honey pouring from a jar, and evoke that same quality of movement as you feel the sensation pouring into the space below.

Use the visualisation to evoke the quality of the movement, this smooth, languid, slow pouring of liquid honey, and the sensation flows into the space below with the same quality of movement. Just as liquid honey spreads out all over the surface of the plate onto which it is being poured, feel that the sensation of the face spreads out all over the floor.

Visualise the way steam evaporates from a recently boiled kettle and, evoking the same quality of movement, allow the vibration of the face to evaporate into the empty openness above. This time, as we feel that the vibration evaporates into the space above, we allow the so-called physical head itself to take the journey with the vibration. So we feel that our head itself is growing upwards, imperceptibly slowly, like a plant growing, just a few millimetres.

The vibration continues to expand into the space above, and we allow the physical head to follow the same pathway. The vibration expands in our feeling-imagination up to the ceiling. The physical head just grows upwards a few millimetres. We don't make any effort. The feeling-visualisation simply takes the physical head with it on its journey.

Don't allow your shoulders to take the journey with your head. Visualise water pouring from a tap. Feel that your arms are like two columns of water, and they pour downwards as the top of your head evaporates upwards.

Feel that in this little contracted space between the shoulders flowing downwards and the head evaporating upwards, one of the favourite hiding places of the apparently separate self is being discovered and exposed: 'I, the fearful one', 'I, the guilty one', 'I, the shameful one'. The separate self is being gently, lovingly flushed out of one of its hideouts.

Gently caress the ceiling with the top of your head. Your arms are columns of water pouring into the ground. Your face on all sides is gently pressed up against the walls of the room, caressing them. And then we visualise that the walls themselves are porous, and we just continue to allow this vibration to expand out in all directions into the empty space beyond the walls.

*   *   *

Feel the vibration called 'my chest'. Feel that it is like a thick, velvety tapestry suspended in empty openness. This sensation is another densely woven fabric, woven out of 'me' feelings: 'I, the one who has been hurt', 'I, the unlovable one', 'I, the lonely one', 'I, the sorrowful one', 'I, the inadequate one'.

This is another favourite residence of the 'separate me' feeling. It's not just one feeling; it is a network of feelings that conspire to maintain the illusion of a temporary, solid, finite, located self. All these feelings are woven together, taking up residence in the chest or heart area, maintaining the illusion of a fragment, a separate self, a hurt self.

Lovingly invite this sensation to expand into the space in front: no violence, no forcing, just a loving invitation. Through visualisation we create the pathway in our imagination, and then we invite the sensation to gently follow this pathway.

As the vibration expands into the space, we feel that the density of the fabric is beginning to loosen. There is more and more space between the threads as it expands into the space. The space percolates into the fabric, opening, loosening and relaxing it, pervading it with its emptiness.

Then we visualise the space behind this vibration and we invite the vibration to expand into the space behind. Go very slowly. Visualise that it's happening in slow motion, millimetre by millimetre, into the space. It's not important how far we expand; it's all to do with the quality of the movement.

Feel that you don't have a back. The back is just empty space, and the fabric of the chest is just expanding into that emptiness.

Now into the space on the left.

Now into the space on the right.

Feel that as the sensation expands it is being permeated by the emptiness into which it is expanding. The sensation is giving up its density as it flows into the empty space.

Now into the space below. Again, evoke the image of liquid honey seeping downwards. Evoke the same quality as the sensation seeps into the space below.

And now into the space above.

Allow the sensation of the belly and pelvic area to come to your attention. It's not quite such a densely woven fabric, but nevertheless it is one of the places where our most ancient 'me' feelings are stored, a place of withholding, where the apparently separate self resists expanding beyond its customary limits, a place where the separate self feels fragile, insecure, vulnerable, a place where it needs to protect itself.

Invite the sensation to gradually expand in all directions into the empty space, and feel the slight density of the vibration being permeated by the emptiness of the space.

Visualise that your legs are like two columns of water pouring into the ground. Your legs are just dangling from the hip joints. Don't superimpose the image of a solid ground beneath you. Just let the water pour into the space below. First visualise and then feel the sensation pouring into the space, completely fluid, effortless, not encountering any resistance.

As the legs are flowing into the space below, allow the top of the head to evaporate like a plume of steam into the space above. Allow the spine to gently follow this movement in both directions, so there is a gentle lengthening of the spine in both directions.

The collapsed spine is one of the favourite places for the apparently separate self to hide: 'I, the fragile one', 'I, the abused one', 'I, the disrespected one'. Feel that in this gentle expansion the 'separate me' feeling is being exposed and expanded beyond its customary limits.

Now stop visualising or feeling anything. Just let experience be exactly as it is from moment to moment.

REALIGNING THE BODY WITH OUR UNDERSTANDING

The separate self on whose behalf most people think, feel, act, perceive and relate is made of a belief and a feeling that what I essentially am shares the destiny and the limits of the body.

With the belief, we feel that what I essentially am has a gender, a nationality, an age. We think that what I essentially am shares the destiny of the body. That is, when the body is born, I am born, when the body moves and changes, I move and change, when the body grows old and sick, I grow old and sick, and when the body disappears, I share its destiny and disappear with it.

With the belief that I share the limits of the body, we think that I start here and stop there, that I share the body's nationality, its gender, its age, its health.

It is inevitable, to begin with, that we explore the sense of separation in our beliefs, but as these beliefs are exposed one by one and discovered to have no experiential foundation, this discovery paves the way for the deeper exploration of the sense of separation in the body, the feeling that I am a solid, dense, located body that walked into this room and is now sitting on a chair.

If we want lasting peace and happiness in all realms of experience, it is essential to take this exploration into the body. In the absence of this exploration, the separate self finds a comfortable hiding place in the body and continues to dictate our thoughts, feelings, activities and relationships from behind the scenes. And we wonder why, in spite of our clear understanding, our actions and relationships betray, over and over again, the presence of a separate self. It is because the feeling of the separate self in the body has not been exposed and clearly seen for what it is that it continues to linger there.

*   *   *

I suggest we start in a sitting position. Evoke, to begin with, the old feeling of being a separate body made out of solid, dense material called flesh and bones. First evoke the feeling, and then allow the upper body to fall slowly forward down to the floor, or as far as is comfortable, being sure to move in a way that is consistent with the feeling. It's not important how far we go – we could go six inches, we could go all the way – but go very slowly.

The only thing that is important is the feeling with which the movement is undertaken. Feel 'I am a solid, dense body', and try to move in a way that is consistent with this feeling. The posture is the movement. Don't go all the way; don't go to the end of the posture. Don't arrive in a fixed position. The posture is a movement, not a position.

When we are two inches away from our limit, the upper body comes back to the sitting position. It's all in the quality of movement. Move in a way that is consistent with the belief and feeling that the body is solid, dense, located.

Now we do exactly the same movement, but before we do the movement with the physical body, we do it in our feeling-imagination. This time, instead of feeling that we are a body made out of solid, dense matter, we visualise and feel that our body is made out of liquid. Visualise and evoke the quality of liquid, runny honey.

Don't just take the image; take the feeling of smooth, liquid honey, and without moving the physical body, in your feeling-imagination, feel and imagine that the sensation called 'my body', made out of liquid honey, flows down towards the floor. Feel the quality of honey pouring out of a jar, and without moving the physical body, visualise and feel the sensation flowing down towards the floor with the same quality of smooth, liquid, transparent movement. Go very slowly. The posture is the quality of our feeling-imagination.

Now we turn the jar the other way up, and the feeling-visualisation of the body flows back up towards the sitting position.

And now, again evoking the feeling of liquid honey, this time we take the physical body with us. Be very careful to move the body in a way that is consistent with this new feeling-imagination. The upper body flows forward, very slowly, made of smooth, liquid, transparent honey. Move, as best you can, in a way that expresses the quality of smoothness, effortlessness, liquidity, transparency.

As the honey reaches the plate onto which it is being poured, it spreads out into a liquid puddle. In the same way, when the body reaches the floor or your knees, it doesn't come to an end. The honey just spreads out over the surface of the floor, melts into the floor. First visualise and then feel the body spreading out all over the floor, seeping in all directions.

Just as the honey doesn't stop flowing on the plate, so the body doesn't really stop moving when it comes to the floor or the knees. We feel that it goes on spreading and flowing. Only a body made out of matter is solid, dense and inert. A body made of Consciousness is a body made of transparency, aliveness, sensitivity, openness. Our only experience of the body is a sensation or a vibration, and a sensation or vibration is never still; it is not solid. It is always more or less gently flowing, throbbing, pulsating.

Now the puddle of honey flows beyond the borders of the physical body and spreads out in all directions, four feet around the body. All around the physical body the puddle of honey flows slowly, almost imperceptibly, in all directions towards the walls.

Now we pick up the plate of honey and pour it back into the jar, and as we do so the upper body flows back towards the vertical position, being sure at every moment to move in a way that is consistent with the smoothness, transparency and liquidity of the honey.

This time we visualise and feel that the body is not made out of liquid but out of vapour or gas. Evoke the quality of steam or clouds, and again with our feeling-imagination only, this cloud is gently blown forward. Don't move the physical body yet.

Visualise and feel that this amorphous, vaporous cloud is blown by a very light breeze towards the floor. It spreads out over the floor. In time, the breeze changes direction and this vaporous cloud gathers back up into the vertical position. Go very slowly. It's all in the feeling quality.

Now we do exactly the same movement, only this time we take the physical body with us. But it's no longer a physical body. So, first take time to visualise and feel the sensation of the body made only of vapour, and then feel a gentle breeze on your back, and the cloud is blown effortlessly forward. Move in a way that is consistent with this feeling-imagination.

Go very slowly. The posture is the quality of the movement. We should barely be able to notice the difference between the first time we did this, with our feeling-imagination only, and this time, when the so-called physical body is also moving. Try to move in such a way that you can barely tell the difference between the two. Be like a cloud in the sky, moving so slowly that to an outside observer it would hardly seem as if we were moving at all…a transparent cloud moving through transparent space.

When the cloud reaches the floor or your knees, it flows into the floor. The floor offers no resistance to it, so the vapour just merges with it, seeps into it.

Now the breeze changes direction. The vapour is gathered up and flows back to the vertical position.

*   *   *

Now we do the same exercise, but with a substance that is even finer than vapour. Go to the sensation of the body, or rather, not the sensation 'of the body' – we never find a body; we find only sensation. Go to the sensation.

In fact, we can go even closer than that. All we know or experience of a sensation is the experience of sensing. Just as we replaced the label 'body' with the label 'sensation', now we replace the label 'sensation' with the label 'sensing'. The experience of a so-called body is no longer a noun; it is a verb. See that just by changing the label, the actual experience itself changes. The sensation is no longer 'something'; it is a process rather than a thing, a process of sensing, not an object sensed.

Now, reach into this experience of sensing with your feeling-imagination and ask yourself, 'Is there any substance present there other than the knowing of it?' Try to find a substance present in the experience of sensing other than knowing.

So drop even the label 'sensing', and see that the only substance actually present in the experience of the body is knowing. Stay with this experience of pure knowing. All we know or come in contact with is this knowing, and it is this knowing that knows this knowing.

Now allow the upper body to fall forward again, but do not know anything other than knowing. As the movement takes place, know only knowing. Be only knowing. Allow the body to move in a way that is consistent with this understanding: knowing moving in knowing.

In fact, knowing is not moving; moving is in knowing. Without actually moving or going anywhere, knowing itself is assuming the form of moving. Move without moving: knowing never knowing or coming in contact with anything other than itself; knowing never going anywhere, for there is nothing other than itself into which it could move or go.

When our head touches our knees or the floor, the head doesn't really touch the knees or the floor. That is simply a concept superimposed on the intimacy of our experience. Knowing simply takes a new name and form; it never comes in contact with anything other than itself. Knowing never goes anywhere. Knowing never knows anything other than itself.

Come back to the vertical position, very slowly.

Now, with this same feeling-imagination, we invite the body to turn to the left. Simply send the invitation and allow the body to respond. Adapt the movement to whatever is comfortable for your body. Again, move in a way that is consistent with your feeling-understanding.

Don't go all the way. This is nothing to do with stretching the body. Resist the temptation to go all the way and complete the movement. There is no completion of this posture. The posture is complete every moment of the way. The posture comes from completion; it doesn't move towards it.

Knowing is the posture, and knowing is always complete and at rest in itself. Knowing never goes anywhere or does anything. There is nothing to accomplish. The movement is already fulfilled. It comes from fulfilment; it doesn't go towards it.

Now invite the head to roll clockwise. Allow the head to fall forwards, sideways, backwards. It's all in the feeling quality. Feel that the sensation is made out of empty knowing…emptiness moving in emptiness. The movement is not moving. Then we reverse the direction of the neck rolls.

Now the wind changes direction and the body turns to the right.

Don't think of this as a series of postures; think of it as movement. Don't reach a conclusion. Don't end in a posture. Don't even think or feel this as movement. All that is known of movement is knowing. All that is known is knowing: knowing knowing only knowing…knowing modulating itself in the form of movement, but never being, becoming or knowing anything other than itself.

Continue with the rolling of the head. It doesn't matter how slow the movement is. It's like a cloud moving imperceptibly in the sky. We feel as if we are not moving: emptiness flowing through emptiness.

Now allow the head to come to the front. Place your hands behind the body on the floor. The head drifts upwards and backwards, and the shoulder blades come closer together.

Feel that the cloudlike sensation is completely pervaded by the emptiness of the space in which it appears. If there are resistances and tensions, just offer them to the emptiness of the space. Let the emptiness pervade the resistances and tensions with itself; let the emptiness transform them into itself.

The cloud comes forward again into the sitting position.

*   *   *

Allow your breath to lengthen and deepen. Feel as if you are an infant breathing in deep sleep: long, slow, deep inhale and exhale.

Now, instead of feeling that the breath is initiated inside the body, feel that it originates outside the body. Feel that the breath is initiated in the space in front of the body, so that the space in front is doing the breathing.

Instead of feeling that the breath enters your body through the nose, feel that it enters your body through its entire front surface. The front surface of your body is like a porous membrane, and the breath originates from the space in front of the body and enters it all over its entire porous front surface.

Then, when we exhale, we exhale through the entire back surface of the body, into the space behind.

The next inhale is initiated in the space behind the body. It flows into the body, through the porous membrane all over the entire surface of the back of the body, pervades and fills the entire body, and then we exhale into the space in front. The next inhale is initiated in the space in front.

We keep breathing like this, back and forth between the space in front and the space behind, all over the entire porous surface of the body.

Now feel that as the breath enters the body over its entire porous surface and fills it, it dissolves part of the solidity of the body and takes the solidity with it as we exhale back into the space. So the density of the body is gradually replaced by the transparency of the breath. The breath carries the density of the body out into the space all around, and dissipates it throughout the entire space.

As we breathe like this, the porous membrane through which the breath flows in and out of the body becomes more and more porous, transparent and open. So as we breathe like this, there is less and less distinction between the emptiness of the breath and the density of the body. Space, breath and body mingle, exchanging their substances with one another.

Now visualise and feel that the space in the room expands in all directions. Visualise a space two or three hundred metres in all directions, in front, behind, to the sides, above and below the body. This entire space is doing the breathing.

Breathe this vast space in and out of the body all over its entire porous surface, allowing the emptiness of the space to percolate into the density of the body, dissolving residues of density, solidity, resistance, tension, 'me-ness'. On the exhale, the transparency of the breath carries the density of the sensation out into emptiness. The density is being saturated in emptiness.

The density of the body expands into the transparency of the space, and the breath is the medium through which this exchange takes place. The body is losing its clearly defined contours.

Visualise and feel that the surface of the body has become so expanded into the space that it's now just a threadbare garment, like a cobweb, separating nothing from nothing.

There's just one space, in which the sensation of the breath and the sensation of the body can no longer be distinguished from each other. And this seamless sensation can no longer be distinguished from the space in which it is appearing.

Now drop the visualisation of physical space. With our eyes closed, we have no knowledge or experience of physical space. Physical space is a concept superimposed on the reality of our experience. Understand and feel that this body/breath sensation is not appearing in a physical space, but rather a knowing space, a knowing space that is not located anywhere. It has no dimensions to it.

This body/breath sensation is completely dissolved into the dimensionless presence of pure knowing.

Just as we allowed the sensation of the body to dissolve into the sensation of the breath, allow this new body/breath sensation to completely dissolve in pure knowing. All there is, is this pure, dimensionless knowing.

No body, no self, no breath, no space, no world: just pure, unnameable knowing.

THE BODY AS PURE, BORDERLESS KNOWING

Allow the experience of the body to come to your attention. Immediately drop the label 'body'. See that, if our eyes are closed (and I recommend we keep our eyes closed, to begin with) the only experience of the body is a sensation or series of sensations.

Ask yourself the question, 'What can I know for certain about the current sensation if I refer only to the sensation itself, and not to a thought, an image or a memory?'

Ask yourself the question, 'How old is the current sensation?' Thirty, fifty, seventy years old? Don't ask thought what it thinks. Thought will tell us that the body is thirty-seven, fifty-two, sixty-eight years old. What does experience say? Go to the actual sensation itself to find the answer to this question. For how long has the current sensation been present?

Does the current sensation have a gender? Again, don't refer to thoughts, images or memories. Thoughts, images and memories are experiences of the mind, not the body. Does the sensation itself have a gender? Does the current sensation have a nationality?

Does the sensation have a weight? Go to the experience of weight; see that the experience of weight is itself a sensation. How much does that sensation weigh?

Is the current sensation sitting on a floor or a chair? Without reference to thought or memory, do we have any experience of a floor or a chair? Is not the apparent experience of a floor or a chair itself simply a sensation that, without reference to thought or memory, cannot be named?

Even to call it a sensation is too much. It is too solid or concrete a name for something that is more like a tingling, amorphous vibration.

Can we find an edge to this vibration, a place where it stops and the space in which it appears starts? In fact, without reference to thought or memory, this vibration is not appearing in a physical space. It's appearing in a knowing space.

Try to find the edge of this sensation. Be very specific. Take your magnifying glass and scan the sensation, looking for an edge or a border, a line that clearly delineates it from the knowing space in which it appears.

See that the sensation is not a sensation 'of the body'. Without reference to thought or memory we have no idea that it is a sensation *of* something. There is no experience of 'a body' apart from the sensation itself. It is just sensation. Stay intimately with the sensation until all that is present is just the current experience: raw, amorphous, borderless, tingling vibration. In this way, allow the sensation to self-liberate itself from all superimposed concepts.

Now we journey into the centre of this vibration. Be like an explorer visiting unfamiliar territory, trying to find out exactly what is there. See that, as we explore this new territory, there are pockets of density and areas that are less dense, some areas that vibrate with an intense frequency and others where the frequency is finer or softer.

Travel with your feeling-attention through the entire landscape of this vibration. Ask yourself the question, 'What is the medium through which my attention is travelling?' Does it travel through something that is dense, solid, opaque? Or is the vibration mostly open, empty space which offers no resistance to our attention?

If we meet areas of density, simply slow down and take time to explore that area. If we meet an area that thought calls 'pain', be aware of the impulse to resist it. That resistance is itself another sensation. Turn towards the sensation called pain rather than away from it. It is just a sensation, a little more intense than other areas but nonetheless simply a sensation. Be the allowing space in which it appears. Travel with your feeling-attention around it and within it. Do we really encounter something solid and dense there?

Ask yourself the question, 'What is this tingling, amorphous, borderless vibration made of? If I had to name the substance that I find there, what substance would it be?'

Keep checking that you are only referring to your direct experience, not to memory, images or thought. All we know about the sensation is our current, intimate, direct experience.

*   *   *

One of the areas where this vibration is at its densest is the area that thought calls 'my face'. Allow the tingling vibration called 'my face' to come to your attention. Drop the label 'face' and just stay with the sensation. Feel that the face is like a mask, about an inch thick, hanging, suspended weightlessly in empty, knowing space.

Explore the sensation intimately. Explore the front surface of the sensation. Can we find a surface there that separates it from the knowing space in which it is suspended?

Visualise and feel that the space in front of the mask is completely open, empty, transparent and without resistance. First visualise and then feel that the front surface of the mask bleeds and merges into this space. We cannot find a place where one starts and the other stops.

Feel the back surface of the mask. First visualise and then feel the space behind the mask. Unless we have a headache, there is no experience of a head; the head is empty. Invite and allow the back surface of the mask to bleed and merge into the open, empty space behind, like a cloud bleeding into an empty sky.

Invite and allow the front and back surfaces of the mask to expand and dissolve into the transparency in the front and behind. Don't contrive or manipulate anything. Simply invite and allow.

Visualise and feel that the eye sockets are empty, like two empty spheres the size of ping-pong balls. Invite and allow these two empty spaces to expand into the space all around. The space inside the eye sockets expands in all directions, seeping into and permeating the sensation of the mask as it goes. The space all around the mask percolates into the sensation, permeating it and dissolving residues of tension.

Feel the density of the area that thought labels 'my nose'. Visualise and feel that the nose is a cavity the size of a walnut. Invite and allow the space of this cavity to expand in all directions, percolating through the sensation of the mask, merging with the space all around.

Feel the tingling vibration that thought labels 'my mouth'. First visualise and then feel an empty cavity the size of a plum. Invite and allow that space to expand in all directions. It's all done with our feeling-imagination.

Allow the tingling vibration called 'my ears' to come to your attention. Visualise and feel two cavities there the size of hazelnuts. Invite and allow these spaces to expand in all directions, blending with the other spaces, percolating through and saturating the tingling vibration of the mask.

Feel that the mask softens, opens and expands. Feel that this vibrating mask has expanded twelve inches into the space in front and twelve inches behind. As it expands, its density thins out.

Invite and allow the expansion to continue another twelve inches in all directions. As the vibration expands, it intermingles with the space, and the space in turn infiltrates and permeates the sensation.

The mask continues to soften, open, expand and disperse. It's now like a vast, gently undulating cloud, four feet in diameter.

And now, feel a gentle breeze on your right cheek, and allow the breeze to blow the cloud to the left. Very slowly, almost imperceptibly, the cloud that thought once labelled 'my head' begins to turn to the left. The cloud moves so slowly that the movement is almost imperceptible. Feel that this huge, soft, transparent cloud is being very gently carried on the breeze.

The cloud is moving so slowly that we barely know that anything is moving. In fact, nothing is moving. Movement is an interpretation. A vibration is simply changing shape within itself; it is not going anywhere. And even that is too much: nothing is changing in the present itself. See that thought evaporates in this understanding, and with it, time, movement, change. There is only the unspeakable reality of what is.

Don't arrive anywhere. The posture is not a position of a body. The posture is the feeling quality.

The breeze changes direction. Feel the sensitivity of the air on your left cheek, and the cloud begins to float to the right. It is carried weightlessly on the breeze. No effort; the breeze does everything. Nothing really moves; only a vibration changes its shape. Don't arrive anywhere. The posture is the movement.

And then the cloud drifts back to the centre.

*   *   *

Scan the tingling, amorphous, borderless cloud and ask yourself if you can find a self anywhere inside it. Is there anything inside the sensation other than sensation? And is there anything to sensation other than knowing?

Allow the vibration that thought labels 'my chest' to come to your attention. This is another area where the vibration is often at its densest. It is rich in feelings: feelings of being hurt, upset, inadequate, guilty, fearful, lonely, unlovable, a failure or having a sense of lack. All these feelings appear in the chest area as a densely woven knot of sensation, mimicking the presence of a separate self.

Visualise and feel this sensation like a blanket hanging suspended in empty space. Invite and allow this vibration to expand into the empty space in front and behind. Feel that the back of the body opens up and the sensation called 'my chest' expands into the space two feet behind… and now two feet in front.

Visualise and feel that as the sensation expands it thins out and is infused and permeated by the space into which it grows.

Now include the sensations in the belly and pelvic area. These sensations are often subtler, less easy to name. They are the areas where our deepest, unnameable, unfaceable feelings of fear, resistance and withholding reside. Invite and allow the density of the sensations to soften, relax, open and expand into the space in all directions.

Now include the legs and the rest of the body.

And now stop compartmentalising the body, and feel that it is just one homogeneous, amorphous vibration expanding in all directions, in front, behind, to the sides, above, below, seeping into the space all around it, and being infused and permeated by that space. The vibration and the space are making love, mingling their substances, merging into one another, losing themselves in one another.

Invite and allow this amorphous cloud of tingling vibration to expand until it touches the walls of the room all around. Feel that the nebulous edges of the cloud gently caress the surfaces of the walls.

And now, while keeping this feeling-visualisation of the entire body expanded to the walls in all directions, seeping into the empty space and being pervaded by it, the breeze wafts the cloud to the left. Slowly, imperceptibly, the upper body turns to the left. We don't really feel that we are moving; the vibration is simply changing shape.

Don't arrive. The posture is the movement, or more accurately, the posture is the quality of the movement. The movement is fulfilled at every moment. The movement comes from fulfilment; it is not going towards it. The movement is made of fulfilment, made of peace.

When the upper body is facing the left leg, it flows forward to cover the leg. Again, we move so slowly that we don't really register any movement. You can extend your legs if you want to. We move so slowly that we're barely aware of the movement. This expanded vibration is just changing shape. The mist is descending on the plain.

No effort: the movement is effected by relaxation, not by effort. The posture is the relaxation. The posture is the transparency.

If new tensions or new densities are evoked by this movement, be aware of the impulse to resist, and do the opposite: welcome them. Invite and allow them to expand in all directions into the empty space. Allow the emptiness of the space to pervade them.

The mist begins to evaporate into the mountains, and the upper body comes back, imperceptibly slowly. A body is not moving; a vibration is undulating.

The upper body flows to the right and slowly falls forward to cover the right knee…and comes back.

Now stop visualising or feeling anything in particular.

*   *   *

Allow whatever sounds are present in your environment to come to your attention. Ask yourself the question, 'What can I know for certain about this sound, based only on my direct, current experience, without reference to thoughts, images or memories?'

Is it a sound 'of something', or is it just a sound? See that we never find the 'something'. We only find the sound itself.

Can we find an edge or a border to the sound, a place where the sound stops and the knowing space in which it appears starts? Is the sound clearly delineated from the knowing space in which it appears, or does it bleed into the space, just as a sensation bleeds into the space?

Is the sound appearing in a different space from the space in which the sensation appears, or is it the same space? Go back and forth from the sound to the sensation.

As our attention travels back and forth from the sound to the sensation, does it leave one space and enter another? Or are they both appearing in the same space, the same knowing space?

See clearly in the intimacy of your experience that these two vibrations that thought labels 'sound' and 'sensation' are floating weightlessly in the same knowing space.

Now try to find the relationship between the sound and the sensation. Can we find an edge where one stops and the other starts? Or do these two vibrations bleed into one another?

Be completely intimate with your experience. Travel from the sensation to the sound and back again. Try to find a line in your experience where the sensation ends and the sound starts. Where is that line? It is in thought, not in experience.

Can we really find two clearly defined objects, one called 'a sound' and another called 'a sensation'? Or is it just one seamless, intimate experience, vibrating at different frequencies?

Is there any part of the space in which the sound appears that is not filled with and pervaded by the sound? Can we find any part of our experience where the sound is absent? Or is the entire field of our experience pervaded by the sound?

Now what about the sensation? Is there any part of the field of experiencing or knowing that is not filled with and pervaded by the sensation?

Instead of calling it 'sound' and 'sensation' we should call it 'sound-sensation'.

Imagine that we are a scientist journeying into the heart of the sound, taking samples of the stuff that it is made of. And then we journey into the heart of the sensation and take samples of the stuff the sensation is made of. We take our samples back to the lab and compare these two substances. What do we find?

We have these two jars in which we have collected the substances out of which the sound and the sensation are made, but the jars are empty. Neither the sound nor the sensation is made out of 'something'. They're both made out of pure, empty knowing: two different frequencies of the same empty, transparent knowing; two different frequencies that, in fact, completely blend and merge with each other like instruments in an orchestra to produce one seamless sound, made of transparent, empty knowing.

At any moment there is always only one experience taking place. It is thought alone that divides that single, indivisible, intimate experience into an apparent multiplicity and diversity of objects called a mind, a body, a self, a world.

Pure knowing knows no such diversity. It only knows itself, modulating itself in all the frequencies of experience; vibrating within itself in all the forms of thinking, imagining, feeling, sensing and perceiving; but always being only itself, knowing only itself and, as there is a complete absence of otherness or separation in its own experience of itself, we can say, loving only itself.

EXPERIENCING THE BODY AS PURE VIBRATION

Allow the sensation of the body to come to your attention. See that it is not in fact a sensation 'of the body'. 'Body' is a label that is added by thought to our experience. It is just a sensation, not a sensation *of* something.

Be like the newborn infant, made of pure sensitivity. All we know of the experience of the so-called body is the current sensation itself. So drop the label 'body' and see that it is just sensation, just a raw, amorphous, tingling vibration, and see that this vibration is suspended weightlessly in a borderless, open, empty space.

The relationship of this vibration to the borderless space in which it appears is similar to the relationship of a cloud to the sky. The cloud is amorphous, changing slowly, floating weightlessly in the sky, with no clearly defined contour or outline. Feel that the body is a tingling, amorphous vibration, suspended weightlessly in empty space.

Now visualise and feel that the entire front surface of this vibration begins to expand into the space in front. This expansion takes place with a similar quality to that with which a cloud expands or evaporates into the sky. The vibration slowly begins to bleed into the space in front. This is all done with our feeling-imagination.

Visualise and feel that this vibration expands into a space about six feet in front of the body. Now visualise and feel that the entire back surface of this vibration expands a similar distance into the space behind.

It is sometimes more difficult to expand into the space behind, because the space there seems to be unknown. There may be some resistance to this expansion. The resistance may take the form of a thought, such as 'I don't want to do this', 'This doesn't make sense' or 'This is not pure non-duality'. Or the resistance may take the shape of a feeling: 'I can't do this' or 'I don't know how to do this'.

These resistances are, in fact, the exposure of an old habit of which we were previously unaware, an old habit of feeling that the body is something solid and dense, made out of matter, located in a particular place. The attempt to expand the body into the space all around confronts this old feeling in a visceral way. It exposes the root of a separate self in the body.

We are not normally aware that we feel solid, dense and located until we make the effort to feel the body in this new way. As soon as we make the effort to feel the body in this way, that is, to expand the sensation into the space all around, the old habit of feeling solid, dense, limited and located is exposed.

So if you feel this resistance, don't feel that your meditation is failing. On the contrary, the yoga meditation is working perfectly! Part of the purpose of this yoga is to reveal the previously undetected feeling of being solid, dense, limited and located. In other words, its purpose is to expose the 'separate me' feeling in the body and then allow it to gradually dissolve. Simply acknowledge the resistance, and gently persevere with the effort to expand the vibration into the space in front of and behind the body.

Now include the two sides, allowing the cloudlike sensation or vibration to bleed into the space on either side…and now into the space above… and now into the space below.

Don't project the idea of a solid, dense, impervious space below the body. With our eyes closed, we have no experience of a solid, dense space underneath the body. All that is there is sensation. It's just empty sky, empty space, and the vibration sinks effortlessly into this empty space, which offers it no resistance.

We may notice that, in spite of our best efforts, we keep springing back, or contracting back, into a familiar way of feeling the body as being solid, dense, well defined and located in one particular place. This is just an old habit that we have been rehearsing for decades, asserting itself over and over again. Every time we notice that we have contracted back into a solid, dense, located object, we gently make the effort to expand the sensation in all directions into the space around.

We have become so accustomed to feeling ourself as a solid, dense, well-defined, located entity that we feel we need to make an effort to expand the sensation in all directions in empty space. We feel that it is natural to be a solid, dense, well-defined entity, and that it is strange or unnatural to feel that we are expanded in all directions in empty space. In fact, it is the other way around. We have become so accustomed to this contracted feeling of the body, as solid, dense, clearly defined and limited, that we have become insensitive to the fact that this contraction actually requires an almost continuous and subtle effort.

We have become so accustomed to this contracted state that we think it is natural, and any attempt to feel the body in another way, in a new way, in a way that is consistent with our new understanding that unlimited Consciousness is the reality of all experience, may at first feel strange or unnatural, and therefore require some effort. This new effort that we seem to have to make to expand the body in all directions is in fact not a new effort; it is the exposure of the old effort that we were previously making in order to contract into a solid, dense, located entity.

One who has been clenching his fist for some time will feel that the contracted fist is the natural position of the hand, and will not realise that he's having to maintain an effort to keep it in that position. When someone asks him to open his hand, he will feel that he has to make an effort to do so. He doesn't realise that the effort to open the hand is in fact the relaxation of the previous effort to close it, of which he was until that moment unaware.

Every time we make the simple and honest effort to expand the vibration of the body in all directions, we are both exposing and eroding this old habit of feeling, 'I am a solid, dense, located entity'. We are erasing a deeply ingrained habit, and each time we make this effort to visualise and feel the vibration expanded in space in all directions, we weaken the power that this old habit exerts on us.

Remember, we are not doing this in order to discover our true nature. We have already recognised our true nature of pure Awareness. We have already made the discovery that what I essentially am is this open, empty, borderless, knowing or aware space in which all experience appears, with which it is known and out of which it is made. What we are doing here is trying to align the way we feel the body with this new understanding so that our understanding doesn't simply remain at an intellectual level but really penetrates the way we feel the body.

Now, we don't only want to feel the body in a way that is consistent with our understanding when the body is in a comfortable, static, relaxed position. We want to feel this way when we're walking down the street, travelling to work, cooking a meal or talking with friends. In other words, we want to feel this way when the body is active, not just when it is passive.

If the peace of our true nature is only accessible when the body is in perfectly peaceful and comfortable circumstances, then that is a fragile peace that is likely to be disturbed by the slightest provocation, for instance when circumstances become difficult or challenging. Such a peace is not the true, imperturbable peace of our true nature.

*   *   *

I suggest that we come to the sitting position. Feel again that the vibration of the body is expanded in all directions, and now this vibration slowly falls forward. The upper body moves forward until it comes to rest on our knees, or whatever is comfortable for us.

Bear in mind that the only important thing is the quality of our movement. It would be fine to move only six inches; how far we move is not important. This has nothing to do with stretching the body. We want not only to *feel* the body but to *move* the body in a way that is consistent with our understanding.

So, first of all, get in touch with this vibration, expanded in all directions, and then this vibration slowly, very slowly, moves into the space in front. We move with the same quality as a cloud expanding into the sky. The upper body falls forward, but the feeling is just this vibration expanding into space.

When the upper body meets the floor, don't superimpose the idea of a solid, dense floor. All that happens is that a new, unnameable sensation appears in Awareness. This sensation is simply another cloud. It is an extension of the vibration of our body. Nothing solid comes into existence. So we feel that this vibration just continues floating into the floor. Feel that the vibration of the body just goes on expanding. Although the physical body comes to a halt, visualise and feel that the vibration goes on pouring into the ground.

Now the vibration floats back to the sitting position, but we don't really have the feeling that 'I am moving the body'. It's rather like a gentle breeze begins to blow, and the cloud is just blown back into the sitting position. Try to feel and move the body in a way that is consistent with that visualisation. We first evoke the feeling of a cloud being blown gently into a new position, and then we come to the sitting position again, moving with that same quality.

In fact, the asana, the position of the body, is not a position; it is a quality of movement. The posture is the quality of movement, not the position of the body. There are no fixed postures in this yoga. The only posture is the quality of the feeling or the movement of the body, and that is a quality of openness, transparency, sensitivity, weightlessness, emptiness. That is the only posture we ever really take in this yoga.

There is no such thing as a static sensation. A static sensation is a concept that finds no correspondence in our experience. A sensation is always gently vibrating, undulating, swelling.

The breeze keeps gently blowing the vibration, and the head falls backwards. We arch between the shoulder blades, and the upper body arcs backwards. Support yourself on your hands, but don't arrive at an extreme. We should always feel, 'I could go a bit farther if I wanted to, but I don't want to'. In other words, resist the conventional yoga attitude of wanting to stretch the body as far as possible. The goal of this yoga is not an extreme posture. The goal is achieved at every moment in the quality of the feeling or movement.

Allow the body to come to rest, and notice how this movement or effort tends to contract us back into the old habit of feeling solid, dense and located. So, once the body has come to rest, expand the sensation again in all directions.

Allow the vibration to expand farther out into space, through the walls of the room. There is no limit to this expansion.

Now this expanded vibration is blown gently back, but it is not just blown back to the sitting position. It's blown all the way forwards again until it reaches your knees or the ground. And then, in a wavelike motion, we curl the back, allow the head to fall forward, and allow the sensation to be blown upright again, and backwards.

We continue to move with this wavelike motion. Evoke the feeling of a wave, and move with the same quality. We are made of water. All the way forward, tuck the head in, curl the spine upwards. The head falls back, the spine arches between the shoulder blades, and then the vibration falls forward again in a rhythmical, wavelike, transparent movement.

We simply move back and forth in this slow, rhythmical way, giving our attention only to the quality of the movement. We move in the same way that a wave undulates on the ocean, liquidity moving in liquidity, transparency moving through transparency.

And then we reverse the direction. If we notice that the movement has tended to contract the body back into a solid, dense, located object, we just pause and allow the vibration to expand again in all directions. Evoke the undulating rhythm of a wave, and then continue the movement.

The body comes to rest in the upright position. Allow the energies that have been stirred up by this movement gradually to come to rest, but don't let them come to rest as a solid, dense, located object. Allow these energies to remain expanded, floating weightlessly in transparent, empty space.

*　*　*

Now allow the sensation of your arms to come to your attention. Feel that the sensation has no border, no outline or clearly defined shape to it. It's just a tingling, amorphous vibration. Let the vibration expand in all directions.

Now, without moving your physical arms, let these imaginary arms made of pure vibration float up to the horizontal position. It's all done with our feeling-imagination. The arms of vibration just hang weightlessly in the horizontal position.

And now these arms of vibration sink back down, but we pay very sensitive attention to the quality of this vibration as it sinks back down into our lap. We do it once more: the imaginary arms of pure vibration float upwards to the horizontal position. It's all about the feeling quality. It's like a breeze moving through empty space, transparency moving in transparency. And now the arms of vibration sink slowly back into our lap, emptiness moving in emptiness.

Now we do it again, and this time we allow the physical arms to take the journey. In theory, there should be no difference in the quality of feeling between the imaginary arms of vibration moving up to the horizontal and the physical arms, because the physical arms are made only of a vibration. Infuse the physical arms as they move with the quality of movement that was present when we were moving only the imaginary arms of vibration. Stay only with the quality of the movement, transparent vibration floating through open, empty space.

When the arms are in the horizontal position, check again that your only experience of the arms is a tingling, amorphous vibration. Visualise and feel that these arms of vibration begin to float forward, expanding into the space in front, until the tips of your fingers touch the wall in front of you. It's all done with our feeling-imagination.

The imaginary arms of vibration expand into the space in front. The physical arms don't move. But we feel that our arms have moved, because all there is to our physical arms is this vibration, and this vibration has expanded and elongated right up to the wall in front, so that we feel that our arms are long vibrations, streaming out into the space in front.

Our imaginary arms of vibration touch the wall in front and our hands caress it gently, like caressing the cheek of our loved one. Very slowly we begin to walk our imaginary fingers of vibration up the wall in front, and as we do so the arms begin to rise. We allow the physical arms to take the journey.

The physical arms slowly begin to rise to the vertical position, but we visualise and feel that our hands and fingers of vibration are climbing up the wall in front. These long streams of vibrating energy are gradually climbing up the wall. At some point our fingers meet the corner between the wall and the ceiling, and then we slowly make our way back across the ceiling, the arms gradually extending into the vertical position.

The posture is the quality of the movement, emptiness moving in emptiness, a current moving in the ocean, made only of water.

When our arms have reached the vertical position we allow the palms of our hands to face the ceiling, and with the hands of vibration we caress the ceiling. Imagine that we are stroking the ceiling very gently. Feel the sensitivity on the palms of your hands, made of pure vibration, tenderly caressing the ceiling. As we caress the ceiling our palms open outwards to the side, caressing the ceiling minutely and sensitively as we go.

Our hands of vibration traverse the ceiling until they come to the corners where the ceiling meets the wall on both sides of the body. Then the palms of vibration come slowly down the wall on either side until they meet the floor.

And then, very slowly, the hands of vibration travel back along the floor to our body, caressing everything and everyone they come in contact with. We imagine that the floor is the head of our cat or the belly of our lover.

We allow the hands to come to rest on the ground beside us. A new sensation appears, but that sensation is just a transparent vibration. There's nothing solid there. Allow the sensation to pour itself into the ground. Visualise and feel two waterfalls streaming down into the earth. The water percolates into the earth. The arms of vibration are like liquid water seeping down into the space below. The earth offers no resistance. All that is there is a porous vibration.

Feel the relaxation in your watery arms and shoulders as the vibration pours downwards into the space below. The water is washing the tensions and contractions out of the shoulders, elbows, wrists, hands and fingers.

*   *   *

Now, keeping this feeling of your arms made of water pouring into the space below, allow the vibration of the head to come to your attention. Immediately drop the label 'head'. All that is there in our actual experience is an amorphous, tingling, borderless vibration. Feel that it is made of vapour, a kind of vaporous vibration, and the vapour begins to expand upwards, like the gently undulating plume of smoke that rises from a recently extinguished candle.

Allow the plume of smoke to take the physical head with it as it goes. The head grows, millimetre by millimetre, upwards as this vapour billows gently towards the ceiling. At the same time, we feel that our watery arms are pouring downwards into the space below.

At some stage our head comes to the limit of its movement, but we visualise and feel that our head goes on floating up like steam evaporating from a boiling kettle. Our arms are made of water, pouring down. Our head is made of steam, floating up.

Our imaginary head of steam goes on wafting upwards until it touches the ceiling. To begin with, just the top of the head touches the ceiling, but then this vibration of the head begins to spread out over the entire surface of the ceiling. Visualise and feel that your head is spreading all over the ceiling above. Our watery arms are pouring downwards, spilling onto the ground and seeping into it, percolating more and more deeply into the earth.

Feel that your legs and thighs are made of water. They pour into the ground. First visualise and then feel that your legs are dangling below you, into the space below, made of water, pouring down into the earth.

Feel that your vaporous head expands through the ceiling into the vast space above, mingling and merging with it.

Now your head, made out of vapour, begins to coalesce and come back down. The water in your arms and legs stops pouring into the earth, and we just come back to the current experience of the body. We stop visualising or doing anything, and just let the current experience of the body be as it is.

The next posture is called everyday life. Just go about your life as normal, but don't be persuaded to think that this yoga meditation has come to an end. The yoga that starts and stops is the yoga of a physical body. The true yoga, the yoga of the transparent body, is not something that starts and stops.

All that happens is an ever-changing flow of sensations and perceptions, made only of never-changing, empty, transparent knowing, made only of our self.

Allow the silence to come to your attention. Although the silence is empty, see that it is appearing in Awareness, appearing in pure knowing. It is saturated with knowing.

Feel that the silence is pervaded by and saturated with pure knowing, and that pure knowing is pervaded with silence. The silence is only the knowing of it. There is no silence apart from knowing. This knowing is silent, empty, transparent.

Everything that appears is like a ripple in this knowing silence, or silent knowing.

Allow the breath to come to your attention. Feel that the breath is like an undulation of this silence. Lengthen and deepen the breath as if you were an infant breathing in deep sleep. Feel that the breath is like a modulation of this ocean of silence.

Abandon the belief and feeling that the breath takes place inside a solid, dense, located body. There is no such experience of a body. There is a vast, borderless ocean of silence pervaded by knowing, and the breath completely fills this empty, silent, knowing space.

The sensation that thought used to label 'my body' is a ripple quivering in the midst of this ocean of breath. The breath is expanded into this empty, silent knowing, completely pervaded by it. The sensation called 'my body' is a quivering ripple vibrating at the centre of this borderless, empty space.

Feel that the breath is not taking place inside a container. The breath is like a mist, completely filling the space in which it appears. It doesn't appear in a physical space; it appears in an empty, knowing silence.

Visualise a landscape in which the space, the air and the mist are one. Now go back to your experience and feel that the silence, the knowing and the breath are one. In this metaphor, the space is pure knowing, the air is silence and the mist is the breath.

Pure knowing is unknowable as an object, completely transparent. Silence, the absence of sound, is the subtlest of all objects. And the breath is a very fine vibration, the first form of silence, like the mist, barely an object, but just discernable. Feel that these three – pure knowing, the silence and the breath – are dissolved into one another.

*   *   *

Allow the vibration called 'my chest' to come to your attention. The chest sensation is slightly denser than the vibration of the breath. It is made of the same stuff, but this vibration feels slightly denser, so dense that it has the feeling of being something solid.

See that there is nothing solid in a sensation, whether it is labelled 'my breath' or 'my chest'. All there is to a sensation is sensing, and all there is to sensing is transparent, empty knowing.

Keep breathing as if you were deeply asleep – long, slow, deep breaths – and with each inhale, feel that the emptiness of the breath seeps into the sensation called 'my chest' all over its entire porous surface. It's like a transparent space seeping into a little dense cluster of mist. The sensation offers no resistance. All there is to the sensation is sensing, and all there is to sensing is knowing. The sensation is a ripple, a modulation, a vibration of this silent, empty knowing.

As the breath seeps into the sensation all around it, feel that it percolates into it, saturating the sensation with its qualities of emptiness and silence. And as this empty, knowing silence percolates into the quivering vibration called 'my chest', the vibration softens, relaxes, opens.

Be sure that the feeling of the breath is completely expanded into the emptiness of pure Awareness, or pure knowing, like a vast, borderless space expanded in all directions, saturated with the breath. It is this silent, empty, aware space that is doing the breathing, and in the middle of this space there is a quivering vibration called 'my chest'. Allow the breath to percolate into this quivering vibration all over its entire surface, seeping into it, infusing its silent, empty substance into the slight density of the sensation.

Then, with the exhale, feel that the breath flows out of the sensation in all directions, all over its entire porous surface, taking a little bit of its density with it, dispersing it into the silent, empty, aware space all around. With the next inhale, the transparent breath seeps a little deeper into the sensation, mingling its emptiness with the fullness of the sensation, dissolving its density as it percolates into it. And with the exhale, the breath seeps out of the sensation and expands into the space all around, taking the density of the sensation with it and dispersing it into the space.

In this way, as we breathe in and out, the transparency of the breath and the density of the sensation mingle more and more intimately with one another. With each inhale and exhale, the transparency, the silence, the emptiness of the breath saturates the density of the sensation with its qualities, dissolving layer upon layer of density as it flows in and out of the sensation.

On the exhale, feel that the breath carries the sensation into the surrounding space, and as it does so the sensation begins to expand in all directions into the space, thinning out as it goes like a cloud evaporating into the sky.

*   *   *

Aeroplane sound

See that the sound is just a ripple in this silence, made only of this silence.

As the sound vanishes, nothing real disappears. All there is to the sound is the experience of hearing, and all there is to hearing is knowing. When the sound vanishes, its reality, pure knowing, goes nowhere. All that is present during the sound is still present now, only it is vibrating at a different frequency.

Feel that the entire sensation that thought once labelled 'my body' is expanded into this silent, empty knowing and is completely saturated with it. There is no part of the sensation that is not pervaded by knowing. In fact, it's not even right to say that, because it suggests that the sensation is one thing and it is pervaded by something else, called 'knowing', like a sponge pervaded by water. It's not like that. All there is to the sensation is sensing, and all there is to sensing is knowing.

The sensation is a modulation, a temporary name and form of silent, empty knowing.

Now we allow a new sensation to be generated by turning the head very slowly back and forth, from left to right. Allow the new sensation that is generated by this movement to come to your attention, but see that no new substance comes into existence. Ever-present knowing takes a new name and form. Silent, empty knowing begins to vibrate at a different frequency.

If we look at the name and form, we believe that something new has appeared, but if we stay with the knowing we see that nothing new has come into existence. In other words, if knowing loses itself in the object, it seems to experience a multiplicity and diversity of ever-changing names and forms, but if it stays with itself it knows only its own ever-presence.

Allow the head to move freely back and forth, but stay with knowing, as knowing, knowing only knowing in the form of this movement. From time to time, stop any movement of the head. See that nothing disappears. A name and form seems to disappear, but its reality remains.

Allow the head to move again. All there is to the head is sensation, all there is to sensation is sensing, and all there is to sensing is knowing. And knowing is not moving or going anywhere: ever-changing sensation, made of never-changing knowing.

Experience is ever-changing when looked at from the outside, never-changing when experienced from the inside.

The sensation is a ripple or a current moving through the ocean, made only of water. The water is not going anywhere; there is nowhere for it to go.

Allow the head to come to rest.

*   *   *

Now, imagine that you very slowly stand up, and your arms start waving about. We do this only with our feeling-imagination, and when we do this with our feeling-imagination alone, the movement of the sensation is completely transparent, because it is made only of feeling, visualising and imagining. There is nothing solid there. Transparent, empty knowing is rippling within itself.

Let the transparent arms move like the branches of a tree in the breeze. All we know is the knowing of them. All there is to the movement is the knowing of it. The movement is the knowing. The movement *is* a new current or eddy appearing in the ocean of knowing, made only of knowing.

Allow this feeling-visualisation to come to an end, and the transparent body sits down again. Allow the energies stirred up by this movement to flow out into empty space in all directions: knowing moving in knowing.

Now we do it again, and this time we take the so-called physical body with us. But before starting, be careful to evoke the feeling quality of the previous visualisation, and infuse the movement of the physical body with this quality.

All we know is knowing, and the 'we' that knows it is knowing itself. Feel that as the so-called body begins to move into the upright position and the arms start to wave about, all that really happens in our actual experience is that this silent, empty knowing vibrates within itself; it takes on a flow of changing names and forms. Don't allow the movement to contract you back inside a physical body. Don't allow knowing to become a knower of the known.

So in our own time, the body comes to the standing position and our arms gently wave around, but we go as slowly as we need to in order to maintain the feeling quality of this contemplation. We keep our eyes closed.

Allow your arms, to begin with, to move completely freely, but we know nothing of 'arms' or 'body' or 'standing up'. I have to use these words to describe the movement, but forget the words as soon as I have uttered them. Know only transparent sensation, flowing in silent, empty knowing.

Know only knowing. Be only knowing. See that our entire experience is only a modulation of that. Feel that these new currents of vibration are completely transparent, flowing like a current in an ocean of pure knowing.

We begin to walk around now. To do this we open our eyes, but don't let any substance other than pure knowing come into apparent existence.

The vibration is now taking the form of seeing. It is becoming a little more colourful. Notice the tendency to contract back into a physical body, to become a physical body moving around in an outside world, but see that nothing really changes. Silent, empty knowing simply assumes new names and forms.

Move as slowly as you need to in order to maintain the feeling quality: silent, empty knowing, vibrating within itself in all the colourful multiplicity and diversity of sensing, seeing, hearing, moving, thinking, feeling, touching. One substance, intimate, indivisible, indestructible, irreducible, never coming in contact with anything other than itself, knowing only itself, being only itself.

The vibration gradually returns to rest on what thought used to call a chair or a floor. Stay with the vibrating sensation, pervaded by knowing, made only of knowing.

Allow the energies that were created by this movement to subside slowly. Feel that the vibration called 'my body' is completely dissolved and expanded into this silent, knowing space. We can no longer find one thing called a sensation, another thing called breath, another called silence and something else called knowing. One substance, ever-changing in name and form, never-changing in essence.

All appearances are temporary names and forms superimposed on or, more accurately, self-assumed by, pure knowing. The essence of meditation, and indeed the art of life, is not to lose sight of this knowing throughout the multiplicity and diversity of experience; to be only this knowing, to know only this knowing and to love only this knowing; not to allow this love to be limited to an object or a person.

THE EMPTY, LOVING SPACE OF AWARENESS

Be knowingly the open, empty, spacelike presence of Awareness in which all thoughts, feelings, sensations and perceptions are appearing.

You, I, Awareness, are equally intimate with all appearances and yet, at the same time, are inherently free of them.

We don't have to practice to make Awareness free of all appearances. We don't have to purify the inherent nature of Awareness. All that is necessary is to see that its inherent nature is already and always open, empty, transparent and free.

Allow the experience of the body to come to your attention. The experience of the body, if our eyes are closed, is just the current sensation. See clearly that this sensation is an appearance in Awareness. If we look inside the sensation, we don't find a little pocket or centre of Awareness; the sensation itself is appearing in the open, empty, spacelike presence of Awareness.

Visualise and feel that this sensation or vibration is suspended weightlessly in this vast, open, empty, borderless space.

Allow the experience of weight to come to your attention, and see that that experience is itself just a sensation. See clearly that, in our direct experience, a sensation has no weight. Any sensation may be more or less intense, but that intensity doesn't give it a weight. 'Weight' is a concept superimposed on the intensity of the sensation.

If someone were to ask us, 'How much does a headache weigh?' we would obviously reply that a headache doesn't weigh anything. However, a headache is simply a sensation like the sensation of our legs on the chair or floor. There is no difference. One is possibly a little more intense than the other, but they are both made of exactly the same stuff.

Go back and forth in your experience between the sensation of your head and the sensation of your legs on the chair or floor. See that they are both equally sensations, one possibly a little more intense than the other. Keep going back and forth between the two sensations until it is clear to you that they are both simply sensations, floating weightlessly in the open, empty, spacelike presence of Awareness.

Take an image of someone that you love deeply, and in your imagination, place that image about twelve feet in front of you. Feel that the space between you and the image of your loved one becomes charged with the love you share.

Now take the same image of your loved one and place it twelve feet behind you. The space behind the body usually feels dark, unknown, but as soon as we place an image of our loved one there, the space becomes charged with the love that we share. So, first visualise and then feel that the space behind the sensation of the body is a loving space.

Place the image of your loved one twelve feet to the left of the sensation, and feel immediately that what was previously an inert space becomes a loving space.

Place the image of your loved one about twelve feet to the right of the sensation, and again feel that the space becomes charged with love.

Place the image twelve feet below the sensation. Don't superimpose the memory of a solid, dense earth below you. Below the sensation it is all just empty space, the open, empty space of Awareness. Place the image of your loved one twelve feet below you in this space and feel that the space is charged with love.

Feel free to use the same image each time, or you can choose different images of anyone you have ever loved or been loved by. The love we share in each of these cases is the same love, so the space all around the sensation is charged with this same love that characterises each of our relationships.

Now we take the image and place it twelve feet above the sensation.

The sensation of the body is now floating weightlessly in a cocoon of love, surrounded on all sides by images of people or animals that we have loved or been loved by. Visualise and feel that the sensation of the body is suspended, held, supported in this loving cocoon.

Now allow the images all around to recede in all directions, and as the images recede into the distance, they colonise the space into which they move with the love you share with them. So this loving cocoon is expanding in all directions. Be sure that it is expanding equally in all directions, including behind and below the sensation, which are sometimes a little more difficult.

See that as the images recede in space, they begin to fade, just as images that appear in time, in the form of memories, also begin to fade. But notice that as the images fade, as they recede in all directions, the love with which the space is charged doesn't fade.

The love is no longer connected to a particular image or person. It is just the experience of impersonal love, without being directed to or from a person. In time the images fade completely, leaving only the sensation, suspended weightlessly in an open, empty, borderless, loving space.

*   *   *

Now, allow the experience of the breath to come to your attention. Slightly lengthen and deepen the breath so that each inhale and exhale lasts three or four seconds. Breathe as if you were a baby sleeping deeply.

See that the actual experience of the breath is just a sensation. All we know of the breath is this subtle sensation or vibration.

Visualise and feel that the breath originates in the loving space in front of the body. Start with the sensation of the face. As we inhale, the breath originates in the space in front of the sensation, it filters into the sensation all over its porous surface, and then, on the exhale, the breath seeps out into the space behind the face.

The face is like a dishcloth hanging on the line, a sheet of vibration, and the breath is like a breeze that is passing back and forth through it, all over its entire porous surface. So we are not breathing through the nose; we are breathing through the entire porous surface of the face. When we exhale into the space behind, the next inhale originates in the space behind. It seeps into the face over its entire porous surface, and then the breath pours out into the space in front, from where the next breath originates.

We breathe back and forth between these two spaces, in front and behind, and the breath is filtered through this porous fabric of the face, all over its porous, amorphous surface. Feel that we are not breathing in inert stuff called 'air'; we are breathing in this loving substance in which the face is suspended. We are breathing love back and forth through the fabric of the face.

Now the breath originates in the space on the left of the face. We feel our left cheek like a piece of muslin hanging on a washing line, feel the sensitivity of the sensation. The breath originates in the space on the left side, it seeps through the porous fabric on the left side of the face, and on the exhale it pours into the space on the right, from where the next breath originates. Then we inhale through the porous fabric on the right side of our face.

This empty, loving substance of the breath flows through the subtle sensation of the head and pours out again into the space on the left, from where the next breath originates. We breathe back and forth like this: long, slow, deep breathing.

Now the breath originates in the space below the head. On the inhale it evaporates up into the porous vibration of the head, permeates the sensation with its empty, loving substance, and then evaporates into the space above, from where the next breath originates.

The next breath originates in the space above, pours down into the head like very gentle rain, percolating into the top of the head all over its entire porous surface, saturating the vibration of the head as it trickles down, and then pours into the space below, from where the next breath originates.

Feel that the density of the sensation of the face and head is gradually and progressively permeated and softened by this loving substance that is being breathed in and out of it.

*　　*　　*

Allow the sensation of the chest to come to your attention. It is a slightly denser piece of cloth, like a tapestry woven out of feelings.

Take some time to become aware of the threads out of which this tapestry is made – feelings, for instance, of being unlovable, not good enough, fearful, ashamed, guilty, lonely, sad, whatever feelings are present, if there are feelings present. See that all these feelings make up this richly woven tapestry, all around the chest and heart area.

Visualise and feel that the breath is initiated in the loving space in front of this richly woven tapestry of feelings, and breathe in this loving substance all over its entire porous surface, feeling that this loving substance percolates into the tapestry and then seeps out into the space behind, from where the next breath is initiated.

If there are some parts of this fabric that are a little resistant to being permeated by this loving substance, then slow down. Put that part of the fabric under the microscope, so to speak. Take time, breathing this loving substance back and forth through this denser part of the fabric where the weave is tighter.

Feel that the breath is initiated in the space on the left, percolates into the sensation all over its entire porous surface, and then seeps out into the space on the right, from where the next breath originates.

Now the breath originates in the space below the sensation, flows through it and evaporates into the space above. If there is any resistance, just see that this resistance is part of the tapestry. The resistance is not a failure of our contemplation; it is being exposed by our contemplation. This resistance is the residue of the separate self in the body, made out of 'me' feelings. It is resisting being permeated by love, resisting opening up to love.

Allow the sensation of the belly and pelvic area to come to your attention. See that the sensation is like a fine piece of fabric, just a subtle vibration. Feel the breath originating in the space in front of this vibration, and breathe this empty, loving substance back and forth between the spaces in front and behind.

Breathe from left to right.

Breathe from the space below to the space above, and from the space above to the space below.

*   *   *

Now stop compartmentalising the body, and feel that the entire body is one quivering vibration. The vibration is perhaps more intense or dense in some areas than in others, but it is one seamless fabric. Feel that the breath is originating in the space all around this vibration.

The vibration is suspended in a vast cocoon of empty, loving space, and this space is breathing love into the vibration all over its entire porous surface. We are not doing the breathing; it is this loving space that is doing the breathing.

With each inhale, feel that the empty, loving substance of the breath percolates into the vibration, finding its way slowly into the depths of the fabric.

Notice if some parts of the fabric seem a little denser, less permeable, resistant to being permeated by this empty, loving substance. Don't force it; just give that particular area more time. Let this more intense, resistant area soak in this loving substance.

As the vibration fills up on the inhale with this empty, loving substance, feel that on the exhale the breath carries the sensation out into empty space with it. So with each inhale, the vibration is permeated by this empty, loving substance, and with each exhale the vibration expands, one inch with every exhale, in all directions.

As the vibration is permeated all over its entire porous surface and filled up by this loving substance, its density is being gradually dissolved, and as the vibration expands into the space all around with each exhale, its tightness is loosened. The density of the vibration is being gently, lovingly expanded into the space all around. The densely woven fabric is beginning to fall apart.

Feel that the vibration of the body is now expanded three feet in all directions, and that as it continues to expand it becomes more and more transparent. The muslin cloth is now more like a cobweb, mostly empty space. The loving emptiness of the breath is turning the vibration into itself, permeating the density of the vibration with its transparent, loving qualities.

As the vibration expands in all directions it becomes less and less easy to distinguish the difference between the vibration and the empty, loving substance of the breath that permeates it. These two substances are mingling, the density of the vibration giving itself up to the transparency of the breath.

The body that started off like a cloud suspended in the sky has dispersed in all directions and is now more like a fine mist that pervades and fills the empty space of the sky. The sky permeates the mist, and the mist permeates the sky. The vibration of the body is fully expanded in all directions and completely fills the empty, loving space in which it appears. The empty, loving space completely permeates and saturates the vibration, turning it into itself.

Now stop visualising anything in particular or controlling the breath. Just allow experience to be as it is.

DISSOLVING BODY, BREATH AND WORLD
INTO PURE AWARENESS

Allow the experience of the body to come to your attention, but immediately drop the label 'body'.

Without reference to thought or memory, we have no knowledge that the current sensation is something called a body. 'A body' is a concept that thought superimposes on the raw, unnameable intimacy of experience.

Come close to your experience. Our only experience of the so-called body is the current sensation. In fact, even the label 'sensation' is a little too well defined, too concrete an object. The actual experience of the sensation is more like a quivering vibration suspended in open, empty space. Know nothing about the vibration other than the actual experience of it in the moment.

See that this vibration doesn't have a weight. Go to the apparent experience of weight, and see that it is itself simply a sensation or vibration. The idea of weight is a concept that thought superimposes on that sensation. That sensation itself is suspended weightlessly in this open, empty space. Don't simply agree with me intellectually; feel that what is being suggested is your actual experience.

Ask yourself the question, 'Does this vibration have a density?' Don't answer the question intellectually. In order to answer the question from our experience we have to dive inside the vibration and touch the stuff that it is made of. When we swim around inside this vibration, do we find something solid, dense, inert? Or is the sensation itself made of a transparent, resistanceless vibration, with nothing solid or dense there?

Wind blowing

Allow the sound of the wind to come to your attention. If I were to ask, 'Is there any density or solidity to the sound of the wind?' we would of course say, 'No, it is empty, transparent.' Go back to the vibration that thought used to label 'my body' and ask yourself the question, 'Why do I feel that the vibration called "my body" is solid and dense and that the vibration called "wind" is transparent and empty?'

Place these two experiences in front of you and go back and forth between them. See clearly that they are made of the same stuff, both of them equally a quivering vibration taking place in the open, empty space of your self. Allow the vibration that thought calls 'my body' and the vibration that thought labels 'wind' to completely mix with one another, or rather, see that they are already mixed with one another. See that there is no clearly defined border between these two vibrations.

Allow the vibration of the so-called body to come to the centre of your attention again. Feel that it is suspended weightlessly in a borderless, empty space. Now visualise someone that you love deeply, and place the image of your loved one in the space in front of this vibration, about eight or ten feet in front of the body.

Feel that the space between the vibration of the body and the image of your loved one is charged with the love that you and your friend share. It's no longer a neutral, empty space; it's a space that is full of the love that you share. Now duplicate the image of your loved one and place it ten feet in the space behind the sensation. This is all done with our feeling-visualisation. There's nothing for thought to do.

The space behind this vibration often seems to be dark or inaccessible. It's relatively easy to feel the space in front, but the space behind often seems to be dense or inaccessible. We don't feel that we can really go there. So now we place this image of our loved one behind us, and immediately we feel that the space behind the sensation becomes charged with the love that we share.

It's like we're standing in a room with our back to the door, and a friend comes in through the door. Without turning around, we become acutely aware of the space behind us. So, feel that the space behind the sensation of the body is charged, full of the love that we share with our loved one. It's no longer a dark, impenetrable, inert space. It is bright with the love that we share with our friend.

Duplicate the image again, and place an image on either side of the vibration of the body. Evoke the love that you and your friend share, and feel that the space between the sensation and these two images on either side is charged with that love. Duplicate the image again and visualise it on the ceiling above the vibration. Evoke the love that you and your friend share, and feel that the space above the vibration is charged with that love.

And now place an image ten feet below the vibration. The space below the vibration often seems to be even denser and darker, more impenetrable, than the space behind. Using thought and memory, we project a solid, dense, impenetrable earth beneath the body. But in our current experience we have no knowledge of a solid, dense, impenetrable earth. This quivering vibration is suspended weightlessly in empty space.

So, first visualise this image of your loved one ten feet below. It's like your dearest friend goes down into the cellar to rummage around through some old boxes, looking for a favourite book. The cellar is no longer dark, cold, empty, dangerous. Your dearest friend is down there, rummaging through old books, and suddenly the space between you and your friend becomes full of the love that you share. Feel that the space between the vibration of your body and the image of your loved one ten feet below is charged with that love.

Now this vibration is surrounded in all directions by the image of our loved one, and the space all around this vibration is charged with the love we share. It's like the vibration is cradled in a cocoon of soft, warm, loving space.

Gradually let the images of your loved one all around fade. The space all around the vibration remains charged with love, but the love is no longer directed to or emanating from an image. The images have faded and vanished, so the vibration is now just suspended in this empty, loving space.

*   *   *

Now allow the breath to come to your attention, but immediately drop the label 'breath'. Without reference to thought or memory we have no knowledge that this sensation is something called breath. The breath is itself simply a sensation or a delicate, quivering vibration, flickering within the larger vibration that we used to call 'my body'. Allow the breath to lengthen and deepen. Breathe like a baby who is sleeping deeply: long, slow, deep breathing.

Now, instead of feeling that the breath is initiated and taking place inside the body, first visualise and then feel that the breath is taking place in the empty, loving space in front of the body. On the inhale, the breath, which starts in the empty, loving space in front of the body, seeps into the body over its entire front surface, not just through the nostrils. We visualise and feel that the front surface of this vibration called the body is porous, made out of a very delicate woven fabric, and the breath seeps into this vibration all over its entire surface.

The breath fills up the vibration, and on the exhale it seeps into the loving space behind the vibration. The next inhale is initiated in the space behind, seeps into the vibration all over its entire porous back surface, fills up the vibration, saturating it with its loving emptiness, and pours out into the empty space in front, from where the next breath is initiated.

We continue to breathe in this way, long, slow, deep breaths, from front to back and back to front, each inhale filling up the vibration, saturating it, drenching it with its loving emptiness, and then pouring out into the space.

The important thing is to feel that we are not breathing dead, inert stuff called 'air' into the body; we are breathing love into it. Love is permeating, saturating the sensation, percolating more and more deeply into it with every inhale, dissolving residues of tension, resistance and withholding, turning everything it encounters into itself.

Now the next breath is initiated in the loving space on the left side of the vibration. It seeps into the vibration all over its entire porous left-hand surface, percolates into the vibration, filling it up with its loving emptiness, and then seeps out over the entire right-hand surface of the vibration, into the space on the right, from where the next inhale is initiated. Keep breathing back and forth between the two sides in this way: long, slow, deep breathing.

The next breath is initiated in the space above the vibration. The only substance present in the breath is this loving emptiness, and on the inhale this pure love pours down into the sensation, permeating the sensation with its qualities, and seeps out into the space below, from where the next inhale is initiated.

Now feel that the breath is initiated in the space all around the sensation, in all directions. It seeps into the sensation over its entire porous surface, percolates slowly and progressively into the slight density of the sensation, mixes its lovingness with this density, and then seeps out again in all directions. As it seeps out, as the breath, made of this loving, empty substance, seeps out in all directions, it carries the density of the vibration out into the space all around. It's like flowing water carrying fine silt in a river.

On the next inhale, the breath seeps into the vibration all over its entire permeable surface, mixes its lovingness with the slight density of the vibration, saturates the vibration with its emptiness and then, on the exhale, carries it out a little bit farther in all directions, into empty space.

Each time the breath, made of loving emptiness, penetrates the density of the vibration, their two substances mingle more and more intimately, the loving emptiness of the breath gradually dissolving any residues of density that are present in the vibration. The vibration, in turn, gives up any density or solidity that lingers to the emptiness of the breath. It's like a cloud evaporating into the sky.

On each exhale, the vibration is carried farther and farther out in all directions into this empty space, so that in time this quivering vibration of the so-called body is like a very faint mist that permeates the entirety of the loving space, and the loving space saturates the entirety of the vibration.

The space is saturated with the vibration, and the vibration is saturated with the loving space. The cloud has become a thin film of mist which fills the sky. The mist fills the sky, and the sky fills the mist. We can no longer tell their two substances apart. There is just this loving emptiness vibrating as the sensation of the body.

*　　*　　*

Wind blowing

The vibration of the body and the slightly finer vibration of the breath have totally merged with one another, and this in turn has merged into the loving space. Now we allow the sound of the wind to join them, just another vibration, vibrating at a slightly different frequency, filling the empty space and itself filled by the empty space – not an inert space but a loving space.

Let the vibration called 'wind' and the vibration called 'body, breath' totally interpenetrate one another.

Now these four substances, wind, body, breath, space, have become so completely merged that we can no longer distinguish one object from another. It's one seamless, intimate, objectless whole. If we were to find a word to describe it, we would write, 'windbodybreathspace'.

Now see that this visualisation of space is in fact itself a subtle superimposition on our experience. With our eyes closed we have no knowledge or experience of space. The visualisation of space is just a concession to the old belief and feeling that the body is an object that appears in physical space.

As a concession to that feeling we use the visualisation of space to begin with, but now drop the feeling that this windbodybreath vibration is suspended in an empty, loving space. It is suspended in an empty, loving, knowing Presence, a dimensionless, loving, knowing Presence. Don't try to visualise that; we cannot visualise or even think about something that has no dimensions. We have to go beyond thought.

This quivering vibration, windbodybreath, is suspended weightlessly in something that is not a thing. It is suspended weightlessly in a Presence that is simply knowing. It is totally loving, allowing, resistanceless, dimensionless.

Feel that the entire substance of this vibration, the windbodybreath vibration, is not only appearing in and known by this loving, knowing Presence, but is made of it.

Now let that part of the vibration called 'my arms' float gently towards the ceiling. Evoke the quality of movement with which a plume of smoke from an extinguished candle rises, and feel that the arms float gently towards the ceiling with the same transparent, effortless quality of movement. Go very slowly, just a millimetre at a time.

Forget about arms; we know nothing of arms. Forget about movement; we know nothing of movement. Stay only with this dimensionless, loving knowing. This dimensionless, loving knowing is the entire substance of our experience. It is going nowhere. It is doing nothing. In the movement, it is not moving. The entire substance of the movement is its motionless, dimensionless, loving Presence.

Knowing is moving through knowing, emptiness vibrating in emptiness, lovingness at rest in lovingness. At every moment this 'emptyknowingloving' is assuming a new name and form, taking a new shape, but not going anywhere or doing anything. It never ceases to know and be and love itself alone.

Wind blowing

Is it the wind that is blowing, the breath that is breathing, the arms that are moving, the body that is sitting? We have no idea. One indivisible, intimate, unnameable vibration, continuously changing its name and form but always made of the same transparent, dimensionless, intimate, loving knowing; never being, becoming, knowing or loving anything other than itself.

The vibration of the arms floats back down again.

Don't do anything. Just let experience be as it is.

POURING EMPTINESS INTO THE BODY

Direct your attention towards whatever thought is present.

Now, direct your attention towards the tingling sensation of your feet.

And now direct your attention to a perception, such as a sound, for instance the hum of the audio system or the faint sound of wind.

In each of these cases we direct our attention towards an object, and by 'an object' in this context I just mean any experience that has objective qualities: a thought, a sensation, a perception. It's like directing the beam of a torch to a series of objects in a dark room. First of all we direct our attention towards the thought, and then the sensation, then the perception. I suggest, at least to begin with, we do this with our eyes closed.

Now, instead of following your attention forwards towards the object, trace it backwards towards the source of attention, the subject. Allow the attention to sink backwards into its subjective source, rather than flowing forwards towards its object.

Notice that although the objects of attention are numerous, the subject of attention is always the same. What can we say from our direct, intimate experience about this subject or source of attention? The first thing we can say is that it is obviously not an object, or it has no objective qualities. If it were an object, or if it had objective qualities, it would be something towards which we could direct our attention. It would be the object of attention, not its subject.

So the subject of attention is sometimes said to be nothing, that is, not a thing, not an object, with no objective qualities. But at the same time, it is that which knows or is aware of our objective experience.

It is nothing, that is, not-a-thing, but it is an aware nothing, a knowing nothing, an aware emptiness. This aware emptiness is called 'I'. It is I that am aware of my thoughts, sensations and perceptions.

When we try to trace our attention backwards or inwards towards its source, we usually start by going inwards into the body. We have this strong belief and feeling that this centre of awareness called 'I' is buried somewhere deep in the head or the chest area.

As such, this empty, aware 'I' seems to be a little space in the middle of the head. Go to the experience of the head – not the conceptual knowledge of the head or the image of the head, but the actual experience of the head that you are currently having. It's just a sensation or a vibration, and we feel that this empty, aware 'I' is located somewhere at the centre of this sensation.

If we stay very close to our experience and trace back our attention to its empty, aware, subjective source, we may start going inwards into the body or into the head, but very soon we discover that this aware emptiness doesn't live there.

*   *   *

Imagine a white piece of paper, an A4 sheet of paper, and the sheet of paper has a hole in the middle of it, about a quarter of an inch in diameter. To begin with, it looks as if the hole is in the paper and that the space of the hole is defined by the shape of the paper. In other words, we think that the space of the hole is a quarter of an inch in diameter.

What's interesting is that when we go up close to the hole, all we find there is empty space, and that empty space doesn't have a dimension; it is not a quarter of an inch. The space that appears to be in the hole is in fact a vast space in which the piece of paper is appearing.

It's the same thing as we trace back our attention to its source. We start going inwards, usually into the head, expecting to find 'I' there. But as we look for this 'I', as we trace attention backwards, it's as if we go through a little hole in the middle of the head. When we pass through that hole into this vast, open, empty, aware space, the space is not in the head; the head is in the space.

This little hole that seems to be in the middle of the piece of paper has the words 'I' or 'I am' written above it. In the same way, the source of attention, that which knows all objective experience, which seems to be located deep within the head or the body, is a little space, a little opening, with the words 'I' or 'I am' written above it.

That 'I' or 'I am' seems to share the limitations of the body; it seems to be located inside the body. But as we approach that 'I', the subjective source of attention, and pass through it, we find ourself in a vast, open, empty space, *as* a vast, open, empty space. It is in this sense that the thought 'I' is the portal through which the apparently separate self passes on its way back home to its true nature.

The experience 'I' is the intersection between infinite Consciousness and the finite mind. The thought 'I', or the experience 'I', is the only experience that the separate self and God's infinite being have in common. 'I' is the hint of God's infinite being in the finite mind.

So, trace back your attention away from its objects, towards its subjective source, which seems, to begin with, to take us on a journey into the body/mind towards a located, limited 'I'. But as we continue that journey, it in fact takes us out of the body/mind, into a vast, open, empty, aware space, or Presence.

Don't try to look for or attend to this aware emptiness. All we could look for or attend to would be an object of attention, not its subjective source. See that the very activity of looking for the source of attention is simply a flow of thoughts that is appearing in that for which it is searching.

The mind that seeks its source is like the fish in the ocean seeking water, like the character in the movie in search of the screen. The mind can never find its source, but at the same time, it can never lose its source; it can never get away from its source. It is swimming in that for which it is in search.

See for yourself, in your own experience, what impact this experiential understanding has on the seeking mind.

When we open a window, the space through which we look seems to be defined by and share the limits of the window frame. But when we go up to that space and explore it, touch it, we find that space has no limits. It is a vast, open, empty space in which the window frame appears. The space is not in the window; the window is in the space. The space itself is never in the view; the view is in the space. The space itself can never be seen as an object, but we cannot say that it is not being experienced.

Likewise, this aware, empty openness is not 'in the view'. In other words, it can never be an object of experience – a thought, feeling, sensation or perception – it is that in which all experience takes place. It can never be known as an object, but at the same time we cannot say that it is not being experienced.

Physical space cannot be seen, but if we were not experiencing it, it would not be possible to see objects. This aware, empty openness cannot be known as an object, but at the same time, we cannot say that we are not experiencing it, or rather, that it is not experiencing itself. If it were not experiencing itself, it would not be possible for there to be experience.

Simply be knowingly this aware, empty openness. Everyone already is this aware, empty openness. That is why I add the word 'knowingly'. Know and feel that you are already this aware, empty openness; no need to become that, no need to practice meditation in order to be that. Simply notice that you may have overlooked this simple fact of experience. Notice that you are that, and simply be that knowingly.

Let the mind do whatever it wants. Let it go wherever it wants to go. Let whatever perceptions appear, whatever sounds, just appear and do whatever they want.

Every thought, every sound, every perception is just like a fish swimming in the ocean. It can never get closer to the ocean; it can never get farther away from the ocean. Nothing we do or cease doing with our thoughts can take us any closer to or farther from this aware, empty openness.

The movement of the fish leaves no trace in the water. The movement of thought and perception leaves no trace on our essential being of aware openness.

To be knowingly this aware, empty openness is to surrender to God's infinite being.

As the separate self passes through the portal with the words 'I' or 'I am' written above it, it ceases to be a separate self. It merges with the true and only self of infinite Awareness, or God's infinite being.

It is in this sense that self-enquiry, or seeking the source of attention, and surrendering to God's infinite being are identical. They are two ways of describing the same non-practice. If we are more intellectually inclined, we may call it self-enquiry; if we are more heart orientated, we may call it surrendering to God's infinite being. Either way, it's exactly the same.

It is in this sense that the paths of knowledge and love are said to be one.

*   *   *

Be knowingly this aware, empty openness. Whatever appears in your experience – whatever thought, feeling, bodily sensation, sight, sound or texture – see and feel that it appears in this openness.

See and feel that whatever appears *in* this aware openness is a modulation *of* this aware openness. Just as waves are only a movement of water, so all thought, sensation or perception is only vibration of Consciousness, a vibration of this aware openness.

Just as the only substance present in a wave is water, so the only substance present in experience is the knowing of it, the awareness of it, Awareness itself. All experience is a modulation of our infinite, self-aware being.

I know this is clear to many of us intellectually, and when I say intellectually, I don't mean that in a disparaging sense. I don't mean to imply that intellectual understanding is not based on real experience; it is. But at the same time, it takes time for our genuine experiential understanding to really permeate the entire realm of our experience, in particular the way we feel the body and perceive the world.

For this reason, we pay more and more attention to the experience of the body and the world, that is, the way we feel the body and perceive the world, in an attempt to align the way we feel the body and perceive the world with our genuine understanding.

Go to the experience of the head. Make sure that you are referring only to your direct, current experience.

You are a newborn infant. You have no knowledge of a past, no idea that you have been born as a body into the world. Your eyes are still closed, and suddenly, in the middle of this openness that you are, a vibration has appeared, a sensation has appeared, which in a few years' time thought will label 'my head'. But the sensation doesn't come with that label attached. It is just an unnameable sensation.

Feel that this vibration is appearing in this empty, aware openness. You are the empty, aware openness in which this vibration is appearing. This vibration seems to have a density to it, in contrast to the emptiness of the space all around it.

Now visualise and then feel that at the top of this vibration there is little opening, a little opening at the top of the sensation called 'my head'. Imagine that you take a bucket and fill it full of the emptiness all around the sensation, and you begin to pour this emptiness into the hole at the top of the head. You pour very, very slowly, and this emptiness seeps into the sensation through this hole at the top.

First visualise it, then drop the visualisation and just feel it. Feel this emptiness pouring, slowly, like clear, viscous honey. It's all done with your feeling-imagination; you feel that this emptiness seeps into the sensation, dissolving the density that it comes in contact with.

Feel that this emptiness seeps down from the top of the head to the region all around the eyes and behind the eyes. This is a region of the head which is rich in 'me' feelings, a place where 'I, the seer' lives, just behind the eyes. Let the emptiness slowly seep into the density behind the eyes, saturating the density with its emptiness, dissolving the density with its emptiness.

Let the emptiness slowly percolate into the middle of the sensation, the place where 'I, the thinker' lives, one of the main residences of the separate self. All that we actually find there in our experience is a vibration, a sensation; this sensation is just mimicking the presence of a separate self. Allow this emptiness to flush the separate self out of its hiding place in the centre of the head; allow the density there to be permeated and saturated by this emptiness.

Feel that the emptiness trickles down through the sensation, through the density in the nose area where 'I, the smeller' lives, permeating it with its emptiness.

Feel that the back of the head is being filled up with emptiness.

This emptiness seeps down into the mouth area, the place where 'I, the taster' lives.

Feel that the head is filling up with emptiness, and the emptiness begins to flow into the throat area, another favourite residence of the separate self.

The emptiness seeps into the back of the neck and slowly percolates into the shoulders. You have the sensation that emptiness is pouring into the body, saturating the body.

It trickles down into the heart area, the main residence of the separate self: 'I, the feeler', 'I, the one who is lonely', 'I, the one who is hurt', 'I, the one who failed', 'I, the one who is unlovable', 'I, the one who is afraid'.

Go very slowly, and take special care to allow this transparent emptiness to trickle gently into all these little places where these feelings reside, all these little vibrations or sensations that mimic the presence of a separate self.

First visualise and then feel – the visualisation is just an aid to feeling; the important thing is the feeling – that this emptiness colonises the density of the sensation, permeates the density of the sensation as it goes, dissolving the density into itself.

The whole heart area is filled up with emptiness, and the emptiness continues to flow downwards into the belly area, a place where those unnameable feelings reside. Feel that the density of the belly cavity is progressively permeated and saturated with this liquid emptiness.

Feel that this liquid emptiness continues to flow downwards and fill up the pelvic and genital area, dissolving any tensions or residues there.

Feel that this emptiness continues to flow down into the legs, filling up the hips and thighs and knees and calves, flowing into our feet and toes, overflowing into our arms and elbows and wrists and hands.

Feel that the body is full of emptiness. There are no thoughts in the body, there are no feelings in the body, there is no self in the body. It's just a gentle vibration pervaded by emptiness.

And when you feel that the sensation is full of emptiness, that the entire sensation of the body is full of emptiness, feel that the emptiness begins to seep out of the pores in the skin. Imagine the skin like a piece of muslin, made mostly of empty holes, and this liquid emptiness begins to seep out in all directions over the entire surface of the skin.

So this emptiness is pouring into the body and seeping out of it in all directions into the space, into the empty space all around. As the emptiness pours through the body, dissolving the residues of separation, it takes these residues and it disperses them in the space all around the body, like silt being carried by a river. This river of emptiness washes through the body, dissolving residues of feeling and tension, seeping through the surface of the skin, pouring out into the space all around.

Emptiness on the inside, emptiness on the outside.

*   *   *

All that remains of the so-called body is this transparent vibration, like a piece of muslin hanging on a washing line, undulating in the breeze. All that remains of a solid, dense body is this quivering vibration, saturated by emptiness, pervaded by emptiness, floating weightlessly in emptiness.

Now, cease doing anything. Just let experience be as it is.

These yoga meditations are a little bit like the scales and arpeggios and studies that a musician practices. The benefits of them are not always immediately discernable but appear later on when we're playing music.

In the same way, we may find, when we're talking with friends during a meal or walking in the countryside in the afternoons, that we suddenly find ourself relieved of the feeling of being located in and as this dense, solid body, that we are this vast openness in which the entire landscape is appearing and out of which the landscape is made.

That is the experience of beauty: everything appears in me, everything is made of myself. When talking with a friend during a meal, the same experience is felt as love.

THE LIMITLESS REALITY OF ALL EXPERIENCE

Whatever appears must appear in something, or on something. It is not possible to have a movie without a screen, it's not possible to have the words of a novel without a white page, it's not possible to have a cloud without the sky. It's not possible to have a thought without…without what?

Moreover, if we are seeing the movie we are, by definition, experiencing the screen. If we are reading the novel we are seeing the page. If we are seeing the clouds we are experiencing the sky. Therefore, if we are experiencing our thoughts – and each of us is experiencing our thoughts – we must, by definition, be experiencing whatever it is they appear in. What is that?

Just as the screen is not made out of the movie, the white paper is not made out of the words of the novel, and the sky is not made out of the clouds, so whatever it is in which our thoughts appear is not itself made of thoughts.

Just as the screen is free of the limited qualities of the movie, just as the white page is free of the limited qualities of the story in the novel, and just as the sky is free of the limited qualities of the clouds that appear in it, so whatever it is in which our thoughts appear is itself free of the limitations of thought and is, as such, unlimited.

The only substance present in the limited movie is the unlimited screen, the only substance present in the limited words is the unlimited paper, and the only substance present in the limited clouds is the unlimited sky. Thus, the screen is said to be the reality of the movie, the paper the reality of the words, and the sky the reality of the clouds – that which is real in them. The movie, the words, the clouds are a temporary appearance of their ever-present reality.

Likewise, the only substance present in limited thought is this unlimited 'something' in which it appears. This unlimited something in which the limited thought appears is its reality. In relation to thought, this unlimited something is called Consciousness: it is present and knowing. A limited thought is a temporary appearance of this unlimited Consciousness.

In other words, thought is not made out of thought; it is made of Consciousness. Ice is not made out of ice; it is made of water. The ice is a temporary name and form of the ever-present water. The water is its reality. When ice ceases to be ice, all that is lost is a temporary name and form, but the reality of the ice – the water – is not lost. It remains present and available, ready to assume the next name and form.

So, when a thought disappears, its reality, Consciousness, doesn't disappear. It simply loses a temporary name and form and remains available, ready to assume the name and form of the next appearance.

As it says in the Bhagavad Gita, 'That which is never ceases to be. That which is not never comes into existence.' That which is not, in this case the independently existing object or thought, never comes in or out of existence. The apparent existence of the thought is a temporary modulation of the ever-present being or reality of Consciousness.

*   *   *

Like our thoughts, our feelings and sensations appear in or on something. Whatever it is in which our feelings and sensations appear is itself free of the limitations of feeling and sensation. By feeling in this context I mean sorrow, shame, guilt, fear, and so on, and by sensation I mean the way we experience the body from the inside, for instance the tingling behind the eyes or of the hands or feet.

Whatever it is our feelings and sensations appear in is itself devoid of feeling or sensation and thus cannot be felt or sensed. There is nothing there to feel or sense; there is nothing objective. And yet, at the same time, we cannot say that it is not being experienced.

Whatever this something is in which our feelings and sensations are appearing is obviously not a thing. It has no objective qualities and is therefore not really something. It is thus said in some traditions to be nothing, not-a-thing. However, it is not nothing. The term 'nothing' is simply a concession to the previous belief in the independent existence of objects or things.

If we believe that things have their own independent existence, then that in which they appear is said to be not-a-thing, or nothing. But from its own point of view, this unlimited something in which thoughts, feelings and sensations appear is not nothing. It is full of its own empty self, full of being and knowing, full of empty Consciousness. It is neither something nor nothing.

This is the real answer to the question that philosophers have grappled with for centuries as to how something comes from nothing. Something does not come from nothing, because there is neither something nor nothing. Something and nothing are both based on the presumption of things. Remove that presumption and the question collapses. Both 'something' and 'nothing' are superimposed by thought on the unlimited reality of all experience: empty, unlimited Consciousness.

This full, empty reality in which our feelings and sensations appear is the same full, empty reality in which our thoughts appear. In relation to thought it is called Consciousness; in relation to feelings and sensations it is called love. Love is to our feelings and sensations what Consciousness is to our thoughts.

If we take any feeling, such as hatred, sorrow, despair or shame, and we stay with it long enough, if we face it fully enough, experience it deeply enough, allow it completely enough, we will always find love at its origin.

The Vedantic path, or the path of discrimination, is a path that starts with the understanding that 'I am not this feeling', and by discriminating in this way we recognise ourself as the loving space in which the feeling appears and out of which it is made.

In the Tantric approach, we don't say, 'I am *not* this feeling'; we say, 'I *am* this feeling'. We allow the feeling fully into ourself. We face it with unconditional openness. We stay with the feeling throughout all its permutations, allowing it to gradually deliver us to its reality, love.

Both paths are equally valid. The exploration of the experience of thought leads to its reality, Consciousness. The exploration of feelings and sensations leads to their reality, love. These two paths are well catalogued in the spiritual traditions. The first is the way of discrimination, Jnana Yoga, and the second, the way of love, Bhakti Yoga.

However, we don't just think and feel and sense; we also perceive. There is a third realm of experience: perception. The exploration of our perceptions is called Rupa Yoga, *rupa* meaning both 'form' and 'beauty' in Sanskrit.

By perception, I mean the way we perceive the world from the outside: sights, sounds, tastes, textures and smells. Sensations are the way we experience the body from the inside, and perceptions are the way we experience the world from the outside.

Just as all thoughts, feelings and sensations appear in and are made of something, which is itself not a thing, so all perceptions appear in something. Whatever that something is, is itself free of the limitations of any particular perception. And whatever this unlimited something is in which all perceptions appear, it is not just the background of perception; it is the reality of perception, the stuff out of which all perception is made.

The stuff that all perception appears in, and out of which it is made, is the same full, empty stuff that our thoughts, feelings and sensations appear in and are made of. In relation to thought it is called Consciousness, in relation to feeling and sensation it is called love, and in relation to perception it is called beauty.

Just as all thoughts are made out of Consciousness and all feelings are made out of unconditional love, all perceptions are made out of beauty. As such, Consciousness, love and beauty are three names for the same reality, in relation to three different realms of experience: thought, feeling and sensation, and perception.

All perception gives to beauty a temporary name and form. All perception is a temporary localisation of the eternal, infinite reality of beauty.

In the words of Shakespeare, 'And as imagination bodies forth the forms of things unknown, a poet's pen turns to shape them and gives to airy nothing a local habitation and a name.' All thought, feeling, sensation and perception give to airy nothing – this full, empty, luminous, loving substance – a temporary name and form.

The finite mind – thought, feeling, sensation and perception – is a temporary localisation of infinite Consciousness, love and beauty. The three forms or three activities of the finite mind – thinking, feeling and perceiving – clothe this airy nothing, this luminous, empty, loving Presence, with their own particular qualities and limitations, making this airy nothing, this luminous, empty, loving substance, appear as thoughts, feelings, sensations and perceptions.

But in doing so, this luminous, empty, loving substance never ceases to be itself. It never becomes anything other than itself, such as an object, person, self or world. It simply modulates itself within its own infinite being, knowing itself in and as the forms of all experience, but never ceasing to be and know itself alone.

*   *   *

Allow the experience of the body to come to your attention.

If our eyes are closed, and I recommend to begin with that we keep our eyes closed, our only experience of the body is a sensation, or a network of sensations. Drop the label 'body' and just experience this network of flowing sensations.

In some areas the sensation is more intense, in others less so, and in some parts of the so-called body there is no sensation at all; it is just empty space. See that the body is never one thing. It is a constantly changing flow of sensations with only the most nebulous form, no clearly defined contour and no weight. The experience of weight is itself simply a slightly intense sensation. That sensation itself doesn't weigh anything.

First visualise and then feel that the body is a tingling, amorphous vibration or sensation suspended weightlessly in this luminous, full, empty, loving substance. By 'luminous' I mean full of knowing, full of that which illuminates or renders knowable all experience.

Now, imagine that in the top of this sensation, the place that thought used to label 'the top of my head', there is a small hole, two or three inches in diameter. Imagine taking a bucket, full of this luminous, empty, loving substance, and we begin to pour this luminous, empty, loving substance through the hole into the sensation.

We first visualise and then feel that this luminous, empty, loving substance is liquid – it has the consistency of water – and we begin to pour this liquid, luminous emptiness into the sensation through this hole in the top of the so-called head.

First visualise and then feel that this liquid, luminous, loving emptiness begins to flow into the skull. Feel that it begins to fill up the cavity in the front of the forehead.

Now this liquid, luminous, loving substance begins to flow into the eye sockets, and just as when we pour water into a bucket with pebbles in the bottom of it, the pebbles are displaced by the water, so as we pour this liquid, luminous substance into the eye sockets, the eyes themselves are dislodged and begin to move around. They are floating in the water.

At some point, this liquid, luminous substance flushes the eyes out of their sockets and our eyeballs spill onto the ground in front of us, leaving just empty spaces in the eye sockets. Feel this liquid, luminous substance pouring through the empty eye sockets. As it pours through them it spills out in all directions, seeping into the space all around the eye sockets.

The membrane around the eye sockets is like fine, porous muslin, and the water just seeps through it. The liquid substance seeps out into the space in front of the eyes, and it seeps backwards into the space behind the head, saturating and drowning the eye sockets in its emptiness, its lovingness. This is all done with our feeling-imagination alone; don't think about it.

This liquid emptiness now pours down into the nose cavity. As it flows through the nose, the nose cavity becomes more and more transparent, more and more empty. This liquid, loving substance seeps out in all directions through the permeable membrane all around the nose, washing out any residues of density or 'me-ness', permeating and saturating everything it comes into contact with, with its emptiness, its lovingness, its luminosity.

This luminous emptiness begins to fill up the space behind the eyes and the nose, the place where all our thoughts supposedly live. Like water poured into a bucket full of twigs, it displaces all the twigs. This liquid, luminous emptiness begins to scatter our thoughts in all directions.

Our thoughts begin to seep out into the space all around through the empty eye sockets, through the empty nose, through the space in the back of the head. Our thoughts are being displaced and jumbled up by the flow of water and transported out into the space all around. They are being drowned by this emptiness.

Keep feeling the continuous flow of this luminous, empty, loving substance pouring into the top of the head, the eye sockets, the nose, displacing all our thoughts, displacing 'I, the seer', 'I, the smeller', 'I, the thinker', flushing it out of its hiding places behind the eyes and in the eye sockets, dispersing it into the space all around.

Feel that the water pours into the mouth cavity, and after some time it begins to loosen our teeth and tongue and eventually flushes them out into the space all around. Feel the cavity of the mouth as a space with no teeth or tongue, this luminous, empty substance pouring through it, cleaning out any residues of 'I, the taster' or 'I, the speaker', permeating the space with its emptiness, turning any residues of density into itself.

This luminous emptiness now begins to fill up the back of the head. The whole of the skull is now full of this flowing water, and this flowing water is seeping out in all directions, all over its entire porous membrane into the space all around. And as the luminous, empty, loving substance per-colates through the membrane all over its porous surface, the surface of the skull, this porous membrane begins to expand in all directions.

Visualise and feel that the whole sensation of the skull is expanding in all directions, emptiness pouring into it through the hole in the top of the head, expanding it in all directions into empty space.

The entire skull is now like a sphere two feet in diameter, its density grad-ually being washed out into empty space in all directions by this liquid emptiness.

*   *   *

Visualise and feel this liquid emptiness pouring into the throat area, one of the subtler hiding places of the 'me' feeling, the 'I' that doesn't have a full voice, that is never heard, that doesn't feel it is able to express itself fully in life. Let this area of resistance or withholding be flushed out of its hiding places in the throat by this torrent of liquid emptiness.

As this liquid emptiness seeps out in all directions over the porous mem-brane of the throat and neck area, it carries these little tensions, these little residues of the 'me' feeling, dispersing them into the space all around, like a river carrying silt as it flows.

Let the torrent of liquid emptiness pour into your shoulders, filling up the whole area of the shoulders in the front and behind, seeping out over its entire porous membrane into the space in all directions, flushing out any 'me' feelings as it flows. This area is one of the favourite hiding places of 'me, the victim', 'me, the fearful one'.

Feel that the liquid emptiness begins to flow into both arms, so that your arms feel like torrents of flowing water. There is nothing solid there, just liquid emptiness pouring downwards like two waterfalls by your sides. Feel that these two waterfalls flow down and touch the ground on either side.

Visualise and feel that your fingers are made of little shafts of liquid emptiness, and they are caressing the floor on either side, spilling onto the ground and then slowly seeping into the ground.

Now this liquid emptiness begins to overflow into the chest area, one of the main residences of the 'me' feeling, one of the densest, richest areas of 'I, the self in the body', where all our feelings of being unloved or unlovable, insecure, unacknowledged, feelings of shame, sorrow and guilt, all seem to substantiate the presence of the 'me' entity in the body.

Feel this cascade of liquid emptiness pouring into the chest area, filling it up with its emptiness, flushing these 'me' feelings out of their customary hiding places, dispersing them in the space all around, in the front, to the sides and behind. Feel that as this waterfall of liquid emptiness flows into the neck, shoulders, arms and chest, they are gradually filled up with its emptiness and begin to expand in all directions into the space around.

If you feel some resistance at some point, that's very good. Don't see this resistance as a failure of your contemplation. It is a sign that it is working. The resistance is saying one thing to us: 'I, the separate self, don't want to be exposed and expanded beyond my customary limits. I want to stay with the known. I want to stay with my familiar reference points, an-chored solidly in space. I don't like this contemplation because it makes me feel insecure. I want to remain in and as a solid, dense, located body.' That is what our resistance is telling us.

The resistance may take the form of a thought, 'I don't want to do this', or a feeling, 'I can't do this' or 'I don't know how to do this'. These are both forms of the same resistance: 'I, the separate self, want to remain in and as a solid, dense, located body. I am happy to *think* that I am infinite Consciousness, unlocated in time and space, but I don't want to *feel* it.'

Offer this resistance – not just the 'I don't want to' but the 'I can't' and the 'I don't know how to' – offer this subtle withholding to the torrent of liquid emptiness. Just abandon it to the emptiness.

Feel this torrent of liquid, loving emptiness beginning to pour down into the belly area, the seat of some of our most subtle and uncomfortable feelings. Feel that your stomach and intestines are washed out and dispersed by this torrent into the space all around, leaving a great, empty cavity in the stomach.

As this liquid emptiness fills up the cavity of the stomach, the stomach, chest, shoulders, neck and arms expand in all directions, so that now the head and the entire upper body are expanded three feet in all directions.

This liquid, loving emptiness begins to flow into the pelvic and genital area. Feel that this area is emptied out of all resistance and withholding, and as the liquid emptiness flows through it, it is expanded in all directions into the space around.

Now the water begins to flow into our legs and feet. Feel this liquid emptiness filling up your thighs, relaxing and dissolving any tensions there, saturating their density with its emptiness, flushing any tensions or withholding out into empty space.

Visualise and feel that the legs are like columns of liquid emptiness pouring down into the earth. They pour straight through the floor, several feet into the earth below. The water carries on pouring endlessly downwards, carrying the sensation of the legs into a vast, empty space below.

Visualise and feel the entire body as one flow of liquid, vibrating emptiness. Let it swell in all directions, expanding six feet into the space all around.

The sensation is never the same. We can never step in the same river twice. It is one constantly changing flow of liquid emptiness, gradually expanding in all directions, merging with the emptiness all around.

The arms and legs are like four columns of liquid emptiness pouring into the earth. The head is like a fountain flowing upwards until it touches the ceiling above. The liquid emptiness of our back begins to wet the wall behind us. The fine, porous muslin called our chest has expanded up to the wall in front, made only of liquid, vibrating emptiness, wetting the wall in front of us.

Visualise and feel that this great mass of liquid, vibrating emptiness is filling the entire room. The edge of the body is the edge of the room, liquid emptiness pouring through it, carrying it on out through the walls of the room. The head expands through the ceiling. The four columns of water called arms and legs merge together into one waterfall that cascades deep into the earth.

Feel that as this liquid vibration expands in all directions it colonises everything that it comes in contact with. It turns everything that it comes in contact with into itself.

Birdsong

The sound of the birds singing is just a little vibration of liquid emptiness appearing in our body, in our body of vibrating emptiness.

Aeroplane sound

The distant roar of planes taking off is just an empty vibration, reverberating in our limitless body.

Feel that the breath is an expanded column of liquid, loving emptiness liberated from the prison of a physical body. It is the entire space that is doing the breathing.

Now cease visualising or doing anything in particular. Just allow the reality of experience to speak for itself.

THE TRANSPARENCY OF THINGS

Allow the experience of the body to come to your attention. In particular, allow the sensation called 'my head' to come to your attention.

The head is one of the favourite residences of the separate self, the place where 'I, the seer', 'I, the hearer', 'I, the thinker', 'I, the smeller' and 'I, the taster' lives.

Allow the tingling sensation of the eyes to come to your attention and, very gently, remove your eyes from their sockets. Put them down carefully beside you. Visualise and feel the empty space of the eye sockets.

Allow your eyes to open, just a couple of millimetres, and see that the image that you now see fills the emptiness of the eyes. Feel that there is nobody doing the seeing. The eyes are simply an opening, an empty space. They are not physical objects. They are not located somewhere. Seeing is not happening somewhere; all 'somewheres' are made only of seeing.

It is on account of the emptiness of the eyes that the fullness of the view is taking place. Feel that the view is full of the emptiness of the eyes.

Allow your eyes to close. Feel that the space of the eye sockets expands so that the eye sockets are now the size of oranges. Allow the eye sockets to keep expanding in all directions.

They are now the size of melons.

Feel that the eye sockets are two huge spheres, three feet in diameter.

Six feet.

Twelve feet. Be sure that the eye sockets are expanding equally in all directions. Sometimes it's more difficult to expand into the space behind.

Now the space of the eye sockets is as large as this room. And then we slowly allow our eyes to open, and we feel that the image that gradually emerges fills this vast emptiness of the eyes.

Feel that the experience of seeing is not taking place here, at a fixed location. Seeing is not even taking place everywhere. 'Here' and 'everywhere' are made of the experience of seeing. Seeing itself takes place in this vast, unlocated openness. Our eyes are the openness which is filled by the world. Our eyes *are* the world.

Feel that whatever we are seeing is completely transparent to the emptiness in which it is appearing.

Do we experience an entity that is doing the seeing?

Is not the visual image that we are seeing completely pervaded by this emptiness? The emptiness is not located somewhere. It is just a vast openness that is filled by the world. The fullness of the world is completely pervaded and saturated with the emptiness of the space of the eyes.

Of course, the materialists would argue that when we close our eyes the world disappears, and that when we open them again it reappears. Moreover, they would argue that we always see the world from the perspective of the body, and that both these facts imply, and indeed prove, that seeing is located in the head.

Imagine a woman called Mary, asleep in her bed in New York, dreaming that she is Jane walking on the streets of London. When Jane closes her eyes, the streets of London disappear. When she opens them again, the streets of London reappear. Likewise, Jane notices that she always experiences the streets of London from the perspective of her body, and she concludes from these two facts, like the materialists, that seeing must therefore be taking place just behind her eyes, in her head.

However, what Jane doesn't realise is that her mind, in this case the experience of seeing, is not located behind her eyes, in her head. Jane's mind is a temporary and imaginary localisation of Mary's infinite mind, which is located in New York. It is with Mary's mind that the streets of London are seen.

I won't say more about that now, because here we are not interested in models and theories; we are interested in our actual experience. But at least this analogy opens us to the possibility, at a rational level, that seeing does not take place in the head, and so answers some of the objections that thought raises. Above all, it paves the way for this deeper experiential exploration that we are presently engaged in.

Understand and feel that the tingling sensation called 'my eyes' is being experienced. It is not doing the experiencing. Feel the relaxation that takes place in the eyes when the experience of seeing is not felt to be taking place at a location by a person.

Allow your eyes to close. The colouring of the emptiness disappears, but the vast emptiness remains.

*   *   *

Allow the sensation of the head to come to your attention. Very carefully remove your brains and place them beside you. First visualise and then feel that the skull is completely empty. It is just a hollow cavity.

Now feel that this hollow cavity begins to expand. Don't think about this. It doesn't make sense for thought. It's all done with our feeling-imagination. Just feel that the whole empty cavity of the head slowly expands like a balloon.

The cavity is twelve inches in diameter.

Three feet.

If you encounter some resistance, don't feel this as a sign of failure. The resistance may take the form of a thought, such as 'I don't want to do this' or 'I don't know how to do this', or it may be simply a feeling of resistance.

Either way, the appearance of this resistance is a very subtle form of ego. It is the separate self feeling that it is being discovered and flushed out of one of its favourite hiding places: 'I, the thinker', living in the brain. It feels that its hideout has been discovered and is being dismantled. The separate self is resisting being expanded beyond its customary limits.

So if we feel some resistance, it's a very good sign. It's a sign that our contemplation is working. I don't mean to imply that if we don't feel any resistance our meditation is not working. It's fine either way. If we feel resistance we can just slow down.

Acclimatise to this new expanded feeling of the head, and when the resistance has died down a bit, just continue to expand the emptiness of the head, inch by inch. It's all done by invitation, no pushing, no forcing or violence.

Six feet.

Twelve feet.

The size of this room.

And out through the walls into the space beyond.

Feel that the head is a vast emptiness. Let your thoughts and images float freely in this emptiness. Set them free from being contained, locked up in a small, solid, dense, located head. Allow them to float freely in this vast emptiness.

Feel that the thoughts are completely transparent to the emptiness. They appear like little puffs of smoke, temporarily colouring the emptiness and then vanishing. There is no one doing the thinking. The thoughts are just abstract configurations of sound, signifying nothing.

When I was a young child I used to lie awake in bed at night, and I would take a single word and repeat it over and over again until it was simply an abstract sound, without any meaning or significance. So take a thought now, one that would normally be meaningful and significant, and repeat that thought several times until it loses its meaning and just appears like a string of abstract, meaningless sounds, like the sound of birds chirping, or the sound of music. The sounds are simply the sounds. Without the corresponding associations they don't mean anything. Experience your thoughts in this way.

See that our thoughts have no binding power unless we consent to give it to them. If we give them that power, they have that power. If we don't, they don't.

*   *   *

Allow the experience of the ears to come to your attention. Visualise and feel two cavities the size of hazelnuts, and allow these two cavities to expand in all directions. Go very slowly. Be very sensitive to any resistance. 'I, the hearer' that lives in the ears is being flushed out of one of its favourite hiding places.

The cavities are the size of walnuts.

The size of apples.

Melons.

Pumpkins. As the space inside the ears grows, feel that the experience of hearing is liberated from being localised inside a head.

Three feet.

Allow the space of the ears to expand beyond the walls of the room and out into empty space.

Aeroplane sound

Feel that the faint sound of the aeroplane is a colouring of this empty space. Feel that what we call 'here' is not a place in space; it is this vast openness.

Feel that there is no one doing the hearing. Feel that the experience of hearing is not located somewhere. The sound of the traffic on the streets of London is not taking place inside Jane's head. It is taking place in Mary's unlocated mind.

From Jane's point of view, the experience of hearing takes place inside her ears. But Jane doesn't *have* a point of view; she *is* a point of view, a point of hearing, in this case. Jane's actual experience of hearing takes place in Mary's unlocated mind.

It is only from Jane's imaginary and, ultimately, illusory point of view that hearing is taking place in her head. It is not Jane who is having the experience of hearing; hearing is taking place in, is known by and is made of Mary's infinite, unlocated mind.

Jane's mind is the agency through which hearing takes place. Jane is the activity of Mary's mind, which takes the shape of hearing. Jane is an activity, not an entity. The ego is a process, not a self.

Allow the experience of the mouth to come to your attention. Carefully remove your teeth and tongue and place them beside you. Feel that the mouth is an empty cavity, and the cavity begins to expand in all directions.

Feel a cavity in the nose. Invite and allow it to expand in all directions. It joins with the cavity of the mouth. Invite and allow the cavity of the nose and mouth to expand in all directions, beyond the walls of the room, out into empty space.

Now the head is one vast, borderless, empty space. Every sight, sound, smell, thought, image is floating freely in this space. They are transparent to this empty space.

*   *   *

Allow the chest area to come to your attention, the place where 'I, the feeler' lives, 'I, the one who is hurt, afraid, lonely, unlovable, ashamed'. This area is really the stronghold of the 'me' feeling.

Imagine an old, crumbling mansion in the Dorset countryside where the remnants of the British aristocracy are still holding out. The drawing room is the last room to be abandoned. The drawing room is full of furniture covered in old, fading velvet. The chest area is full of old, velvety feelings: thick, rich, dense, tenacious.

The chest area is the drawing room of the separate self. In spite of all the old, worn furniture with its faded, threadbare covering, the musty smell, the peeling pain, the separate self likes to stay there. Its identity is deeply invested in this location; it feels comfortable there.

So, go to the chest area and remove its contents very carefully: the heart, the lungs, the ribcage. Take it all out. We are removing the sofas, the chairs, the tables, the curtains. Place the contents of the chest area beside you. Feel the empty cavity of the chest area and allow it to expand, gently, carefully, sensitively, into the space all around. We simply invite the empty cavity of the chest to expand into the space. We visualise and then feel it expanding into that space, no forcing, no pushing.

As the space of this cavity expands in all directions, feel that all your feelings are liberated from the cage in which they have been living all these years. Don't try to get rid of any feelings; don't touch the feelings themselves. Leave them completely free. The cage in which these feelings have been contained is expanding, and they are happy to have more room in which to move around.

Feel that the skin all around the chest, in front and behind, has expanded and is touching the walls of the room on all sides. We feel that the skin is gently pressed up against the wall in front. Feel the temperature there on your skin. Our back is leaning gently against the wall behind.

Whatever feelings are present, if indeed there are feelings present, have been liberated from the confines of a solid, dense, located body and are now able to move around in this new freedom, this new emptiness. And then the emptiness of the chest area expands through the walls in all directions.

Now allow the belly and pelvic area to come to your attention. This is the cellar of the old house, the place where all the old, damp boxes and trunks have been stored for generations. Many of them haven't been opened for decades. It is the place where some of our subtlest, deepest and darkest feelings reside. They haven't seen the light of day, haven't seen the light of Consciousness, for years.

Remove all the organs in this area and place them gently beside you. Invite and allow the empty space of the belly and pelvic area to slowly expand in all directions. Allow any tension or withholding to be gradually expanded into the space.

*   *   *

Now go to the experience of the skin. The skin is just a thin film of sensation that seems to separate the empty space on the inside from the empty space on the outside. Gently take off your skin and carefully fold it up, placing it beside you. Visualise and feel that there is no difference between the emptiness on the inside and the emptiness on the outside. Indeed, there is no longer an inside and an outside.

Our thoughts are free to go wherever they want in this vast, empty, borderless space. Our feelings are free to expand beyond the confines of a solid, dense, located self.

Allow your experience to be self-liberated from the tyranny of a separate self living inside the body. The world is your body.

Somebody asked me recently what it is like sitting up here on this platform. I have no experience of sitting up here on a platform. I, in this context, am the only thing that is *not* being experienced. It is all of you that fill the emptiness of me. All there is of me is a few sensations and thoughts floating around. It's ninety-nine per cent you, ninety-nine per cent world.

Feel your experience in this way. Feel that it is on account of our emptiness that the fullness of the world exists. Our emptiness *is* the fullness of the world.

Now visualise the world, and slowly remove everything. First of all, visualise removing all the people. Now remove all the buildings. Remove all the animals. Remove all the trees, the flowers, the fields, the mountains, the seas. Remove the sun, the moon, the planets. Remove everything until there's just a vast, empty space.

Ask yourself the question, 'What is the difference between the empty space of my mind, the empty space of my body and the empty space of the universe?' When all objects have been removed, where is the difference? Are there three separate empty spaces?

We are this vast, borderless emptiness. This emptiness is our irreducible, indestructible nature. See that when we start to replace everything that we have taken out of this vast space, nothing actually happens to the space itself.

When we replace our thoughts, they are colourings of this empty space. They are made of this empty space but they don't modify the space itself.

Aeroplane sound

The sound of the aeroplane is transparent to the space.

Whatever feelings are present are colourings of this space. They don't modify the space itself. The real content of the feelings is the space itself.

Having emptied ourself of all experience, and knowing that we are this irreducible, indestructible, empty field of pure experiencing, allow the fullness of experience to return. But see that as it returns it is only a modulation of this emptiness itself. Every experience is completely transparent to the space in which it appears.

The emptiness of the space has no need to defend itself against or resist any appearance, because every appearance is simply a colouring of itself, a vibration of itself.

If we ask what it is that is vibrating in the form of our thoughts, feelings, sensations and perceptions, the only substance we find there is this emptiness.

Cease visualising or doing anything. Simply allow experience to be as it is.

THE GARDEN OF EXPERIENCE

I suggest that, at least to begin with, we keep our eyes closed for this contemplation.

See clearly that all we know or could ever know is experience: thoughts, images, memories, feelings, sensations, sights, sounds, tastes, textures and smells. Even when our eyes are closed, although we can't see the world, there is still a kind of orangey-brown image of the back of our eyelids.

Allow the full range of experience to appear to you just as it is from moment to moment, and very lightly visit each experience in turn, that is, each thought, image, memory, feeling, and so on. Start with a thought. Take any thought – it doesn't matter what its content is – and just, as it were, visit the thought.

Now, take an image. Again, it doesn't matter, the content of the image; it could be your bedroom or kitchen or sitting room. Just visit the image with your attention.

Now take a memory. Visit the memory. Take an expectation, some event that you imagine may happen in the future. Just visit it.

Now take a sensation in the body, that is, the tingling sensation of, say, the hands or the face. Visit the sensation. Now visit the reddish-brown image on the inside of the eyelids.

Visit whatever sounds may be present, the sound of a bird calling or the passing traffic. Visit whatever you might be touching, the chair or the texture of the fabric on which your hands are resting.

Now visit whatever other experiences may be taking place.

See that all these are taking place in the same field of experience.

Now we go back to a thought again. Take any thought, irrespective of its content, and imagining that you are a little particle made out of experiencing, go to visit that thought.

And now, as this particle of experiencing, we move from the thought to an image. Take the image, for instance, of your kitchen and just move with your attention from the thought to the image.

Now allow a memory to come to your attention, and as this particle of experiencing we move from the image to the memory…and now from the memory to an expectation…and now from the expectation to a feeling…and now from the feeling to a bodily sensation, for instance, the tingling at the soles of your feet.

In each case, we are not doing anything to the experience we visit. We are simply visiting each one, like a butterfly going from one flower to another in a garden, alighting briefly on each flower and then moving on to the next. As this particle of experiencing, we are moving from flower to flower, from experience to experience, briefly tasting or knowing each one as we travel.

Now move from the sensation to whatever sounds are present…from the sound back to a sensation, for instance, the tingling of our hands…from the tingling sensation back to a sound…from the sound to the reddish-brown image on the back of our eyelids…from the image to a thought.

Now just allow this particle of experiencing to roam freely over the entire field of experiencing, visiting briefly each experience and then moving on. We allow the butterfly to go wherever it wants: memories, feelings, hopes, fears, perceptions, images.

Ask yourself the question, 'Do I, this particle of knowing or experiencing, ever encounter anything outside of experience? Do I ever leave the field of experience in order to come in contact with a thought, memory, image, feeling, sensation, sound, or do I always stay within the field of experience?'

Now ask yourself the question, 'As this butterfly is going from one flower to another, does it ever encounter any edges or borders or boundaries?' When it is moving, for instance, from a thought to a sensation, does it leave one field called 'the mind' and enter another field called 'the body'? Does it ever encounter a boundary between the mind and the body?

Indeed, does it even encounter something called a mind or a body, or does it just fly effortlessly through the field of experiencing, from the thought to the sensation?

And when this butterfly, the particle of knowing or experiencing, goes from a sensation to whatever sound is present, does it leave something called 'a body' and enter something called 'a world'? Does the butterfly encounter some kind of border between a body and a world? Does it leave one and enter the other? Does it ever come across an object called a body or a world, or does it just find a flower called 'the tingling sensation' and another flower called 'the sound of traffic', both blooming in the same garden of experience? Does this particle of knowing or experiencing not simply flow effortlessly from one object to the other?

When the butterfly moves from the sound to a thought, does it leave one kind of space called the world and enter another called the mind? Does the particle of pure knowing or experiencing ever encounter a border between a world and a mind? Does it ever encounter an object called a world or a mind? Or does it just fly freely and effortlessly through the borderless garden of experience?

See that the thought that divides the garden of experience into three separate categories – the mind, the body and the world – is itself simply one strange flower blossoming in the same garden. That thought doesn't actually divide experience into three separate parts. There are only separate parts from the point of view of thought. For the butterfly, for the one that knows or experiences, there is just one garden. Everything is taking place in the same garden of experience.

See that as the silences between my words get longer, old habits of thought and feeling may begin to return, feelings of boredom, restlessness, irritation, expectation.

Thought says, 'Okay, that meditation was very nice for a minute or so, but now I want to get back to my usual business.' Its usual business is wandering away from the now into a remembered past or imagined future. But see that even these thoughts that seem to wander away from the now never truly leave the garden of experience.

These feelings of boredom, restlessness or expectation are all just strange flowers growing in the garden. They don't take place outside the immediacy and intimacy of experience. There is no outside of experience. The butterfly never leaves the garden.

Keep checking in experience that we never enter a mind to know a thought, we never leave a mind and enter a body to know a sensation, and we never leave a body and enter a world to know a sound. It is all one garden, one borderless field of experiencing.

*   *   *

Now, allow your eyes to open, but no more than a millimetre. Allow them to open as little as possible, and see that the reddish-brown image is replaced by a new colour. A new flower blossoms in the garden, and the butterfly goes to taste it or know it, but it never leaves the garden.

We never leave the field of experiencing and enter or know an outside world. Whatever we know or encounter is always within the field of experiencing.

Now go from the sight to a thought…from the thought to a sensation… and from the sensation back to the image or sight of the so-called world. In doing so, see clearly that we never leave a world and enter a mind, we never leave a mind and enter a body, and we never leave a body and return to a world. We always remain in the same garden; we always remain in the same field of experiencing.

Now see that we are not really like a butterfly visiting flowers in a garden. We are not really a particle of knowing or experiencing, visiting objects in the field of experience. We are the field itself.

Understand and feel that whatever experience you encounter is encountered within yourself. Our self is not any particular object that we encounter. It is the entire field of experience in which all objects appear, with which they are known and, ultimately, out of which they are made.

The attention which we direct towards each object in turn is itself made out of the empty field of experiencing. Our attention is simply a directing of that field towards an object within it.

One of the things I am frequently asked about is, 'I understand everything you say when my eyes are closed. It is obvious to me that thoughts, bodily sensations, the sounds which I once considered to be at a distance from myself, are all experienced as close, intimate. It is obvious to me that I am the open, empty, aware field in which all experience appears, with which it is known and out of which it is made. But as soon as I open my eyes, a self seems to contract inside the body and a world is simultaneously projected outside.'

So, let us explore this discrepancy between our experience with our eyes closed and our experience with open eyes.

The visual realm is the one in which apparent duality is at its most persuasive. It is for this reason that in most cases it is the last realm of experience to be colonised by this understanding. So, unlike most of our other contemplations, we keep our eyes open for this one.

Begin by looking at any object – a flower, a table, a lamp, a chair, a tree, a cloud – and simply look at the object in a conventional way, with a feeling that 'I am located here, in and as the body, and the object is located over there, in the world, at a distance from myself'. This is all about feeling and seeing; there is nothing for thought to do.

Feel that as you see the object, something in you goes out from the body in here, towards the object over there. It's a movement from me, here, to it, there. In other words, we are invoking the conventional, dualistic way of seeing an object.

Try to be aware of the very subtle effort that is involved in this way of seeing. It's as if we go out of ourself to grasp the object.

And now, whilst looking at the same object, gradually relax any effort in the looking. Relax the tension in the attention that you give the object: attention without tension. Instead of going out towards the object, we let the object come to us. Nothing changes in *what* we see, only in the *way* we see.

Be very sensitive to the relaxation of the effort to grasp the object. We are just pure sensitivity, pure openness, pure experiencing, without direction, motive or agenda. We allow the object to come to us; we do not go towards it.

Now we relax the focus of our attention from any particular object and we give the entire visual scene the same quality of attention, a completely relaxed, unfocused looking or seeing. In fact, we no longer look at the object; we simply see it.

Be very sensitive, and distinguish the difference in your experience between looking at something and simply seeing it. Go back and forth between these two experiences. Don't look at a particular object; just see the entire view equally, as if you were looking at one painting, rather than a multiplicity and diversity of objects.

Now, instead of giving your relaxed attention to this global view, give your attention to the experience of seeing itself. Nothing changes outwardly. What we see doesn't change, but the way we see changes. We are no longer interested in the seen object but rather in the experience of seeing itself.

Go back and forth between these two experiences, from the seen object to the experience of seeing itself.

If we are looking at the seen object out there we are, without realising it, identifying ourself as a located subject in here. It is not possible to have an outside world without an inside self, or an inside self without an out-side world. These are two sides of the same coin.

Now go back to the experience of seeing. Nothing changes outwardly. What we see doesn't change; only the way we see changes. Ask yourself the question, 'Where does the experience of seeing take place?' Does see-ing take place 'over there' or 'in here'?

Understand clearly that the experience of seeing doesn't take place in a place. Our only knowledge of 'place' is itself made out of the experience of seeing. We cannot even say that seeing is taking place everywhere, be-cause our only knowledge of 'everywhere' is itself made only of seeing.

In this way, understand that both 'somewhere' and 'everywhere' are con-cepts superimposed by thought on experience. We cannot even say that seeing is taking place nowhere, because 'nowhere' only makes sense in reference to 'somewhere' and 'everywhere'. If we see that 'somewhere' and 'everywhere' are concepts superimposed on the intimacy of our experi-ence, we understand that 'nowhere' is similarly a concept.

We cannot even say that seeing is unlocated, because 'unlocated' only means something in reference to the idea of an object that is located. As a legitimate concession to that belief, we might say, as a provisional for-mulation, that seeing takes place nowhere, or seeing is unlocated, but even that is not quite true. The idea that seeing is taking place nowhere or is unlocated is simply a thorn that removes a thorn.

The understanding that seeing takes place nowhere is a thorn that removes a previous thorn, that is, a previous belief, that objects that are located somewhere, or everywhere. In reality we cannot name the placeless place, the dimensionless Presence, in which seeing takes place.

*   *   *

If someone were to ask us to reach out and touch the seen object, such as the flower, the tree, the table, the chair, we would all know exactly what to do. We would reach out our hand, touch the object and feel what it was made of. But what if someone were to ask us to touch the stuff that seeing is made of?

Don't simply think about this. Reach out an imaginary hand made of pure sensitivity, pure knowing or pure experiencing, and touch the stuff that seeing is made of. If we are experiencing seeing we are, by definition, experiencing the stuff of which seeing is made. What is that?

Do we find anything that resembles dead, inert matter, or do we find this completely alive and transparent substance called knowing or experiencing?

Ask yourself the question, 'What is it that knows the experience of seeing?' Whatever it is that knows the experience of seeing is obviously what we call 'I'. Each of us has the experience that 'I am seeing'. 'I' is that which knows the experience of seeing. What is the relationship between this knowing 'I' and the experience of seeing?

Is the experience of seeing known by a little fragment, a particle of knowing, sitting in the corner of the field of seeing? Or is the entire field of seeing pervaded by the knowing of it, the experiencing of it? In fact, to say that the entire field of seeing is pervaded by the knowing or experiencing of it suggests that seeing is one thing and the knowing or experiencing of it is another.

See if you can find these two elements in experience: one, the experience of seeing, and two, the knowing of it. If someone were to ask us to first go to the experience of seeing, and then go to the experience of the knowing of seeing, would we not go to the same experience? Are not seeing and the knowing of seeing the same experience?

Understand that if we stay close to our intimate and direct experience, we cannot separate the seen object from the experience of seeing, and we cannot separate the experience of seeing from the knowing of it. In our actual experience, the seen object, the experience of seeing and the knowing of it are one and the same. They are three names for one reality.

If we look at an outside object from the perspective of an inside self, we seem to see something called matter.

If we look at the experience of seeing itself, we seem to know something called mind.

And if we know only the knowing of experience, then we know only knowing, or pure Consciousness.

In other words, matter, mind and Consciousness are not three separate substances. They are ways of seeing, not objects seen.

To see a world made out of matter is to see in a particular way. To see experience made out of mind is to see in another way. And to know only knowing or pure Consciousness is to know in another way.

It is like looking at our family photos on a laptop. We can say, 'I see my family', or we can say, 'I see an image' or we can say, 'I see the screen'. Family, image and screen are not three separate things. They are ways of seeing, not objects seen. In one, we see objects and selves, that is, we see matter. In the other we see subtle objects, that is, mind. And in the third we see only the screen. These are three names for one reality.

If we see objects and people, the reality of what we see will seem to be finite stuff called matter. If we see events and states, the reality of what we see will seem to be temporary stuff called mind. But if we know only knowing, the reality of what we see will be experienced – that is, will experience itself – as eternal, infinite Consciousness alone.

That is what William Blake meant when he said, 'If the doors of perception were cleansed every thing would appear to man as it is, Infinite. For man has closed himself up, till he sees all things thro' narrow chinks of his cavern.'

If we close ourself up in the body, if we believe and feel that what we essentially are lives in and shares the limits and destiny of the body, everything we know and perceive will be conditioned by and appear in correspondence with that belief. The world will be reduced to a multiplicity and diversity of objects made of dead, inert matter, and all people will seem to be separate and at a distance from ourself. As a result, a pattern of desire and aversion will characterise our relationship with everything and everyone around us.

Liberate experience from the tyranny of an inside self. Finite objects and selves are ways of seeing, not things that are really seen. All that is really seen is seeing, and all that is ever known of seeing is the knowing of it. All that is ever known is knowing, and it is knowing that knows knowing.

Be only knowing. Know only knowing. Love only knowing. See that the entire garden of experience is only that.

OFFERING THE BODY TO LOVING EMPTINESS

In our conversation last night we saw that we never actually find an object called 'a thought'. Take, for example, a thought such as, 'What shall we have for dinner tonight?' When the 'What' appears, the 'shall we have for dinner tonight?' is absolutely non-existent. When the 'shall' appears, the 'What' and 'we have for dinner tonight?' are non-existent. We never actually find a thought.

We could say it's just a series of words appearing, a series of sounds, but even that isn't quite right. If we take the word 'dinner', when the 'd-' appears the '-inner' is non-existent. And when the 'i' appears, the 'd-' has disappeared and the '-nner' has not yet come into existence. But what about the 'i' itself, or the '-nner'? It's just a sound.

What is a sound? Try to find something in your experience called 'a sound'. Do we ever find a nice, neat package of experience called a sound?

It's just hearing. And what is hearing? Don't say, 'I don't know'. You are experiencing hearing. You must be experiencing the stuff it is made of. What is there?

And what about the experience to which the word 'dinner' refers? It's just a collection of tastes, smells, sounds, sights and textures. Have you ever found a neat package of experience called 'a taste' or 'a smell'? Have you ever been able to capture a smell, put a border around it and say, 'This is an object, this is a noun, this is a thing?' Does a smell, a taste, a sound or a sight ever stay still for long enough to acquire the existence of a thing? Does the experience ever become a thing?

Are there any things, any clearly defined objects in experience? Or is it just a flow of seeing, hearing, touching, tasting and smelling?

But wait a minute. What about this flow? If experience is flowing, it must be flowing through something, through something we call 'time'. Try to find this stuff called time.

Time is the duration between two events. The duration between now and breakfast is what we call 'the past'. The duration between now and lunch is what we call 'the future'. Try to experience the past. Try to cease experiencing the now, in other words, leave the now and actually visit the space we call the past. Don't think about it; experience it. Can you go there?

Feel the immensity of this space that is supposed to exist just behind the now, which contains our entire history – our childhood, our education, our relationships, our activities – this vast space in which our entire life is supposed to have taken place. Where is that space? Can you find it? Can you step out of the now and visit that space?

And what about the future, the place where all our hopes and dreams and desires are expected to manifest? Try to go there. Try to visit the space we call 'the future'.

Bring yourself in this way to the experiential understanding that we never experience time. Time is a concept, not an experience. How would it be to live without the belief in these two vast spaces, the past and the future, unless those concepts were required provisionally for practical purposes?

What does this tell us about the now? Normally the now is considered to be a moment, a sliver of time, sandwiched between these two vast spaces extending indefinitely behind us and in front of us. Is that our actual experience?

Do we experience such a thing as a moment, a present moment? Try to find this package of time called the present moment. How long does this moment last? And how could a moment last if there is no time present for it to last in?

See that the now has no dimension. It has no duration in time. There is no time present in which it could last. There is no time present through which the now is travelling. The now hasn't come from the past and it's not going towards a future.

Now is eternity.

Don't try to think of eternity. If we try to think of eternity we immediately turn it into an object. Thought conceives of eternity as everlasting in time. Thought is just superimposing its own limitations on eternity, believing that it lasts forever in time. Eternity doesn't last forever. There is no 'ever' in which it could last.

If we think that the present moment lasts a second, then we can say, 'No, it's actually half a second in which experience takes place', and then, 'No, it's a quarter of a second', an eighth, a sixteenth. We go on back and back and back until it becomes clear that the now doesn't even last for a nanosecond. There is simply no time present in which the now has duration.

This understanding should really confront the mind with its own absurdity, the absurdity of the projections that it has created and believed to be true.

*   *   *

What about the place at which all experience takes place? All experience obviously takes place *here*. Strangely, wherever we are, it is always here. We go looking for the 'there', and when we get there, it is here. There is no distance from here to there. It is always here.

Like the past and the future, the 'there' is this vast space in which our experience is believed to appear, and yet which nobody has ever found. Try now to find the place we call 'here'. Most of us will go to a vague feeling of the body. Here is roughly this circle of a couple of feet in diameter. But where exactly in that sphere is here?

Go a little more deeply, take your magnifying glass out, and try to find the actual place that is here. Reduce the diameter of this sphere from two feet to one foot as you try to localise here, and then from one foot to six inches. Can you find a place called 'here'? Is here a tiny point moving around in a vast three-dimensional space? Everything apart from this tiny point here in this vast three-dimensional space is called 'there'. But we never find the 'there'.

The here is not a tiny point in space, just as the now is not a moment in time. The here has no dimensions; it is infinite, meaning not finite. It has no finite dimension. All experience takes place now and here. We can't even say experience takes place *in* the now and the here. There is no dimension to the now, here, in which experience takes place.

This entire four-dimensional experience that we have is birthed out of something that has no dimensions. Don't try to think of that. If you try to think of it, it will just short-circuit your mind, just blow your mind. That's what nirvana means: 'blown out'. When the mind touches its source, touches the stuff out of which it emerges, the mind collapses into the dimensionless Presence out of which it is born.

As the finite mind is born out of this dimensionless Presence, it gives birth to space and time. Space and time are the mind. It is this dimensionless Presence itself that assumes the appearance of time and space. Time is birthed out of eternity, space is birthed out of infinity.

The Big Bang is the emergence of time and space from this dimensionless Presence. This dimensionless Presence is called 'I'. It is what we find at the very heart of ourself. If we go deeper and deeper and deeper into ourself, through all the layers of thought and feeling and sensation, there is just this dimensionless Presence. All experience emerges from that.

The common name for this dimensionless Presence is 'I'. The religious name for it is God's infinite being.

God's infinite being dreams time and space into apparent existence. Time is what eternity looks like from the point of view of one those dreamed characters. Space is what infinity feels like from the point of view of a dreamed character. But the dreamed character is just a point of view, not a viewer. It is a localisation of God's infinite mind, a window through which God is able to view a segment of its own infinite potential.

In Shakespeare's words, 'And as imagination bodies forth the forms of things unknown, the poet's pen turns to shape them and gives to airy nothing a local habitation and a name.' All experience 'bodies forth' from airy nothing, from God's infinite being, giving God's infinite being 'a local habitation and a name', enabling God to realise a section of its own infinite potential. Each of our minds is, as it were, an image in God's dream.

The other common name for this dimensionless Presence is love. In the experience of love, the divisions and distinctions that seem, from the point of view of the finite mind, to be so real dissolve, leaving us in our shared being, this being that is whole, complete, indivisible, that cannot be added to or taken from.

The creation is love manifested. It is crystallised love.

In the words of E. E. Cummings, 'Love is a place, and through this place of love flow, with brightness of peace, all places. Yes is a world, and in this world of yes live, skilfully curled, all worlds.'

Feel that your experience comes saturated with the love out of which it emerges. Feel that every experience of thinking is pervaded by, saturated with this empty, loving substance. Feel that whatever feelings may be present, if there are feelings present, are held, cradled, pervaded by this empty, loving substance out of which they appear.

Even our most painful feelings – sorrow, loss, despair – are ripples of feeling bathed in the loving emptiness in which they appear. Don't touch the feelings; just offer them to this loving emptiness. Let the loving emptiness take care of them.

*   *   *

Feel that the experience of the body is only a sensation. Now try find that thing called 'a sensation'. Can you find a neatly packaged parcel of experience called a sensation? There is nothing there called a sensation; it is just sensing, and sensing is just vibrating.

What is the stuff that is vibrating? What is there? It is just this airy nothing, this loving emptiness vibrating within itself.

Feel that the sensation is permeated with the loving emptiness in which it appears and out of which it is made. It's one thing to understand this with the mind. It is quite another thing to feel the body and perceive the world in a way that is consistent with this understanding.

Understanding dissolves the mind, and love dissolves the body. Offer your body to this loving emptiness.

Feel that the vibration out of which the body is made is swimming in the loving emptiness in which it appears. Totally give up the sensation to the space. Allow the emptiness of the loving space to infiltrate, saturate the sensation.

Visualise this loving emptiness like a vast, empty space. Feel the sensation or vibration over the entire front surface of your body: your face, neck, chest, belly, pelvic area and genitals, your thighs, your shins, the upper surface of your feet. Feel this vibration like a delicate piece of muslin suspended weightlessly in this empty, loving space.

Visualise first, and then feel, that the vibration begins to expand into the space in front. Go very slowly, and don't think about this. It's all done with our feeling-imagination.

Feel that the vibration is expanded just twelve inches into the space in front. Allow the vibration to keep expanding into the space in front… two feet…three feet…four feet.

Feel that the vibration touches the wall in front of you. Feel the cool of the glass windows pressed up against the entire front surface of this vibration. And then the vibration melts through the glass windows and into the space beyond.

The vibration is mixed with the wind, and the wind carries the vibration across the fields. All the time, the vibration is expanding and thinning out as the breeze carries it across the fields.

Eventually the fine, threadbare piece of muslin comes to rest on the hills on the opposite side of the valley. The breeze deposits the piece of muslin on the grass, and you feel the entire front surface of your body just resting on the cool, damp grass.

Now, leaving the front of the body completely expanded into the space in front, resting on the hills on the other side of the valley, take the vibration over the entire back surface of the body. Visualise and feel that it seeps into the empty, loving space behind.

Feel that you are leaning against the wall behind you, resting the sensation on the wall. And then the sensation seeps through the wall into the space behind. Feel that as the sensation expands into the space behind, it thins out and is gradually and increasingly permeated and saturated by the loving space into which it is expanding.

Eventually the vibration comes to rest on the hills in the distance. You feel the entire sensation like a breeze resting on the hills.

* * *

Feel the vibration called the head. See that in your experience it is just a vibration. Visualise and feel that the vibration begins to evaporate upwards into the space above. Visualise a candle flame that has just been snuffed out, and a plume of smoke rises from the wick. Visualise the pathway of the plume of smoke, and now follow that pathway with the vibration.

As the vibration evaporates upwards it expands and thins out. It touches the ceiling and spreads out all over the ceiling. Then it percolates through the ceiling into the space above.

The vibration mingles with the space above, expanding into it. It becomes one of the clouds. Your head is a cloud floating in the sky.

Your body is the breeze blowing over the hills.

Feel that your legs are like a waterfall. Visualise the waterfall pouring downwards into the earth, and then feel your legs in a way that is consistent with this visualisation.

Notice how adaptable and amenable the sensation of the body is when it is liberated from its prison of matter. Notice how susceptible this vibration is to being felt in a new way. If we feel that our legs are made out of solid, dense matter, then that's how they seem to be. As soon as we replace the image of solid, dense matter with the feeling-visualisation of a torrent of water, and we try to feel the legs in a way that is consistent with that visualisation, immediately the sensation obliges. The legs become liquid. They pour into the ground, pour into the space beneath us.

Feel how relieved the body is to be released from its prison of matter, how readily and happily it takes on this new form – transparent, empty, flowing, sensitive – how readily it merges with its environment.

Feel that your arms are like shafts of sunlight. Stretch out these shafts of sunlight and caress the fields on the other side of the valley. Feel that your fingertips are like little rays of light, stroking the grass.

Feel that the body made of matter is broken open and spread out through the immensity of space. Let whatever feelings may be present escape the prison of a dense, solid body. Feel these feelings – your sorrow or loneliness, the feeling of being ashamed or unlovable or ugly, feelings of fear or guilt or grief – just let these feelings out of the body. Let them float in the space. Don't touch the feelings. Let them be exactly as they are. Just let them expand into the space. Let the space soften them and care for them.

Now, having added the dimensions of time and space to our experience in order to help us feel the body in a way that is consistent with our understanding, let go of the qualities of time and space.

Let all experience return to the dimensionless Presence in which it appears and out of which it is made, the intimate, indivisible, unnameable reality of all experience.

THE NOW IS 'I AM'

Ask yourself the question, 'When does my experience take place?'

The answer is always, 'Now'.

When we had our first day at school, it was now. When we started our first job, it was now. When we had our twenty-first birthday party, it was now. When we had breakfast this morning, it was now. As we are listening to this, it is now.

What is the difference between all these 'nows'? How many nows have you experienced today? Have there been many nows? And if so, how long, exactly, does each now last? Don't think about this. Your experience is taking place now, so now is available for direct investigation. How long does now last?

Is the now that was present while we were having dinner last night a different now from the now that is currently present? And if so, what is the difference between them? When did the now in which dinner last night took place end, and when did this present now begin?

If there is no difference between them, then it means that the now that was present at dinner last night and the now that is currently present must be the same now. If the now in which dinner last night took place and this current now are the same now, then neither can be located in time. Therefore, the now has no limit. It has no duration. It is not in time.

This now is the only now there is. It has no limits; it has no borders; it doesn't start and stop; it is not a moment in time.

This now hasn't come from somewhere; it hasn't come from a distant past. It has not been slowly moving along in time for millions of years to arrive at this moment. This now is the only now that ever is or has been. This now has never been in the past. It hasn't come from somewhere and it is not going anywhere. It has never existed in a past and it is not moving along a line of time into an endless future.

The now is still. This now, the only now there ever is, remains always the same. It is not coming from a past or going towards a future.

Thought cannot think of the now, because thought can only know an object. The now has no objective qualities with which it could be limited, and therefore it cannot be thought about. When thought thinks about now, it turns the now into time.

In order to think about something we must label it, and by the time we have labelled any thing, the thing that we are labelling has already passed. Therefore, it is not possible to label our current, direct experience now. Only an object or event in the past or future can be labelled. In fact, it is not objects in the past and future that are labelled; it is the labelling of our experience that creates the imaginary past and future in which those objects and events now seem to appear or take place.

When we begin to read a novel, the entire novel is present, but the mind cannot read the entire novel at the same time. Thought needs to read the novel in time, although the entirety of the novel is always present now.

It is not the limitations of the novel but the limitations of thought that make the entire novel inaccessible at every moment. Although the entire novel is, as it were, eternally present now, thought can only access it in time. It is the limitations of thought that turn the eternally present novel into a story in time.

Likewise, our entire experience takes place now. Everything we have ever experienced takes place in this now, the only now there is. Nothing took place in a past and nothing will take place in a future. The universe didn't start millions of years ago. There are no 'millions of years'.

Nor will time last forever; there is no 'forever'. There is only eternity, and by the word 'eternity' I am not referring to some remote and extraordinary realm that only certain mystics have access to. I am simply referring to this now, the only now there ever is, this timeless now that each of us is intimately experiencing.

Filtered through the finite mind, eternity appears as time. Thought superimposes its own limits on the eternal now and makes the eternal now appear in a way that is consistent with its own limitations. That is, it makes eternity appear as time. Thus, what is for thought everlasting in time is in reality the eternal now, or eternity itself.

It is not possible to think of eternity. If thought tries to imagine eternity, it will superimpose its own limits upon it and will construe eternity as everlasting in time, rather than ever-present now. In fact, if the mind really tries to think about eternity, or the eternal now, it will bring itself to its own end.

That is why Shantananda Saraswati said, 'Real thinkers don't think.' That is, people who use thought to go to the reality of experience will find that thought naturally, spontaneously and effortlessly comes to an end. This ending of thought is called understanding.

It's very easy to check this in one's experience. When a moment of understanding takes place, the line of thinking that preceded it must, by definition, have come to an end, because if the investigating line of reasoning that preceded understanding had not yet come to an end, then the experience of understanding itself would not yet have been possible.

So, understanding never takes place in thought; it always takes place at the end of thought. When thought comes to an end, time comes to an end. Therefore, understanding never takes place in time. It is for this reason that a line of reasoning that investigates the nature of reality is itself a profound form of self-enquiry or self-investigation. It is a means by which thought follows itself to its own end. It brings itself to its own end.

*   *   *

What else is consistently present in the now? Thoughts, sensations and perceptions always come and go. They are not consistently present; they are intermittent. Therefore, thought, sensation and perception are not inherent in the now. The now is always present. In fact, the now is not always present, because the word 'always' implies a line of time in which the now is continuously present. But in the now there is no time, so we could say the now is eternally present.

Only something that is also eternally present could be inherent in the now. The only element of experience that is eternally present is the experience of being aware, or Awareness itself, which shines in each of our minds as the knowledge 'I' or 'I am'.

Now is not a moment in time. It is our very own being. It is the simple experience of being aware, or Awareness itself. Being aware, or Awareness itself, is eternally present now. The now *is* being aware. Being aware is now.

The now is 'I am'. The now is Awareness or Consciousness itself.

Time is Consciousness objectified by thought. The stuff that is being objectified is pure Consciousness, that is, eternity. It is Consciousness itself that is assuming the form of the finite mind, and in doing so its own eternal nature is appearing to itself, through the agency of the finite mind, as time.

Eternity, or the eternal now, has no dimensions. Pure Consciousness is, literally, without dimensions. In order to appear as the single dimension of time, Consciousness must freely assume the form of the finite mind. In other words, the dimensionless reality of pure Consciousness appears as time in the form of the finite mind.

* * *

Now, ask yourself the question, 'Where does my experience take place?'

The answer is always, 'Here'.

When we were playing in the garden as five-year-old children, our experience was taking place here. Our first day at school took place here. Dinner last night took place here. Breakfast this morning took place here. Our experience now is taking place here.

Ask yourself the question, 'How many "heres" have I experienced today?' Have you experienced innumerable heres? Or is it always the same here?

If every point in space, when it is experienced, is here, then here cannot share the limits of any particular place in space. Therefore, here itself cannot have any limits. It is not something that appears in or at a particular place. As such, it is not finite. It is without limits, or infinite.

Go now to the place where your current experience is taking place. Try to find that exact place. Don't say that you don't know it; each of us knows that our experience is taking place here. 'Here' is the name we give to the place at which experience is happening, therefore we must know or experience whatever it is we refer to as here. What is that? Can we find it at a particular place or point in space?

Allow your eyes to open, and ask yourself the question, 'Where does the experience of space take place?' Does the experience of space take place over there, at a distance from ourself, here? Or is the entirety of this expanse of space experienced here?

Obviously, all of space is experienced here. It is never experienced anywhere other than here. So, here is not a point or a place in space, but rather, space appears here.

Allow your eyes to close again. Ask yourself the question, 'Have I ever had an experience that did not take place here?' If all experience takes place here, that is, if nobody has ever experienced or could ever experience anything other than here, what validity is there to our belief that 'over there', that is, distance in space, really exists?

Ask yourself the question, 'Is there anything in my experience that is consistent with the experience of here?' No thought, sensation or perception is always here, and therefore they are not inherent in the experience of here. Is there anything in our experience that cannot be separated from the experience of here? Only being aware, or Awareness itself.

Now ask yourself the question, 'Can I find a distinction between the experience of here and the experience of being aware – pure Awareness or Consciousness itself?'

See that here is not a place in space. Here is identical to the experience of being aware. Here *is* pure Awareness or pure Consciousness itself, which shines in each of our minds as the knowledge 'I' or 'I am'.

Here is where I am, and that 'where I am' is not a place in space. The answer to the question 'Where?' is always 'Here', just as the answer to the question 'When?' is always 'Now'. Here is pure Consciousness. Here is what I am.

* * *

Just as time is eternity filtered through thought, so space is infinity filtered through perception. That is, just as pure Consciousness itself assumes the form of thought and makes its own eternity appear to itself as time, so pure Consciousness freely assumes the form of perception and thereby makes its own infinity appear as space.

Thus, the finite mind – and by 'the finite mind' in this context I mean thought and perception – brings time and space out of eternal, infinite Consciousness into apparent existence. It is eternal, infinite Consciousness itself that freely assumes the form of the finite mind, thereby making its own eternal, infinite nature appear to itself as time and space.

Time is eternity filtered through thought. Space is infinity filtered through perception. Time is eternal Consciousness objectified by thought. Space is infinite Consciousness objectified by perception.

Dimensionless Consciousness expands, as it were, to become a single line of time, and that single line of time expands to become three dimensions of space. But time and space are always made out of the same eternal, infinite Consciousness, the Consciousness that knows itself in each one of us as the experience 'I' or 'I am'.

If we forget, or overlook, the true background and substance of experience, pure Consciousness, time and space are conceived in its place and are themselves considered to be the background or container of experience. It is for this reason that in our world culture we believe that the universe appears in time and space. Thus, time and space are conceived as two vast, empty containers that mimic the true, dimensionless container of experience.

Having overlooked the true, dimensionless reality of all experience and invented the two substitute realities of time and space to replace them, we then have to manufacture two substances to fill time and space. Events that appear in time are considered to be made out of mind, and objects that appear in space are considered to be made out of matter. Mind and matter are considered the offspring of time and space.

We can only continue to believe in the reality of mind and matter – that is, the inside self and the outside world – as long as we believe in the reality of time and space. But if we explore the reality of time and space, we find just our own self-aware being. It finds itself in us, as us.

Consciousness is the stuff out of which time and space are made. If we look at Consciousness from the point of view of mind, or through the lens of mind, we see time. That is, if Consciousness itself assumes the form of mind, it sees itself as time. However, if Consciousness looks at itself without the filter of the finite mind, then Consciousness knows itself as Consciousness alone. In order to know itself as space, Consciousness must freely assume the form of perception.

It's like three people sitting on a sofa watching television. The first sees a landscape, the second sees a movie and the third sees the screen. They are all seeing the same thing, but the way they see dictates what they see.

Time and space, mind and matter, are ways of seeing or knowing, not experiences or objects that are actually known or seen.

All that is ever known or experienced is pure Consciousness, and it is pure Consciousness alone that knows pure Consciousness.

*   *   *

Now let us try to make this a little more experiential. Allow your two hands to come together, and immediately drop the label 'two hands'. See that the experience of two apparent hands is, in fact, a single sensation.

The newborn infant, made of pure sensitivity, pure knowing, would have no idea that this single sensation or vibration will later be conceptualised as 'two hands'. So, take some time to allow the sensation itself to be liberated from the superimposed belief.

For the newborn infant, made of pure sensitivity or pure experiencing, this vibration is not appearing in either time or space. The newborn infant has no knowledge of time or space. All it knows is the knowing of its experience. The only substance present in the newborn infant's experience is knowing. This knowing is the substance of both itself and its entire experience, although for the newborn infant this knowing has not yet been separated into a self and an object experienced. There is just seamless, indivisible, irreducible, intimate knowing, and this knowing is vibrating in the form of the sensation that thought will later conceptualise as 'my hands'.

Now allow your hands to separate, just a couple of inches. Drop the label. Notice that it is still just a single sensation.

Again, take some time to allow the new sensation to be liberated from superimposed beliefs. It is just a single vibration.

Ask yourself the question, 'How much distance is there between a sensation and itself?' Obviously, none. Ask yourself the question, 'Is there any space in this sensation?' See in this way that the concept of space is superimposed by thought on the sensation itself.

Now allow your hands to move six inches apart. Drop the label. Allow the sensation to be liberated from any superimposed beliefs. Experience the single sensation, in which there is no space.

Twelve inches apart. It is a single experience taking place in the eternal now, the infinite here.

Now place your hands on your knees or legs. See clearly that again we are only experiencing a single sensation. There are no borders or edges dividing this single sensation into a multiplicity and diversity of objects.

Gently rub your left hand on your knee or leg. It is still a single sensation. Now, stop rubbing your left hand on your left leg and start rubbing your right hand on your right leg: still a single sensation.

Now, stop rubbing your hand on your leg and ask yourself the question, 'What is the stuff that took place between the first event – rubbing my left hand on my left leg – and the second event – rubbing my right hand on my right leg?' What is the stuff that is present between these two events?

Time is the name of the substance that seems to take place between these two events. The two events seem to take place *in* time and to be separated *by* time. However, at every moment our experience is of a single sensation. That single sensation appears in Consciousness, not in time.

In order to believe that experience takes place in time, we have to overlook the reality of our experience and resort to thought, in the form of memory. It is only by using thought, in the form of memory, that we conceive time as the duration between these two sensations. There was no time present between these two sensations.

The two sensations are, in fact, not two sensations. It is a single sensation appearing in Consciousness. In dividing the intimacy of our experience into two apparent parts, we overlook its reality. It is as a result of this overlooking of the reality of our experience that the true substance and container of experience, pure Consciousness, is replaced with time.

*   *   *

Allow your eyes to open, and imagine taking a snapshot of what you see. We print that snapshot and stick it on the wall. The snapshot is one image, not ten thousand things. It represents a single experience, not an experience of many things.

Now look at your left hand. Take a snapshot of it, print it out and stick it on the wall. It is a single experience. Look at your right hand, take a snapshot, stick it on the wall. It is a single experience. At no point in our actual experience do a multiplicity and diversity of objects ever come into existence.

In order to believe in a multiplicity and diversity of objects, we must first conceptualise 'a hand'. We must extract an object called a hand from the seamless intimacy of all experience and separate it from everything else.

Now look at your left hand again, and instead of seeing a single image in which there are no discrete objects, see specifically your left hand. And now look at your right hand, and ask yourself the question, 'What is the substance between these two objects?'

It is called space. But in order to believe that we experience space, we must first conceptualise these two objects, our hands. We must first divide the seamless intimacy of our experience into a multiplicity and diversity of objects. In other words, we must overlook the reality of experience. Only then does a substance called matter come into existence, appearing in and separated by stuff called space.

Now allow your eyes to close. Go back to the experience of the hands, but immediately drop the label 'hands'. Allow the sensation to be liberated from the belief and, more importantly, the feeling that you are experiencing two objects in time and space, and see that there is just one seamless, intimate, indivisible experience, made only of pure knowing.

The so-called hands are a single, seamless vibration, and the only stuff present in this vibration is pure knowing, pure Consciousness, our self.

Now, place one hand on the chair or floor. Allow the experience to liberate itself from the superimposed belief that this experience comprises two objects, a hand and a chair or floor. Feel the sensation until it is clear that it is a single, seamless, intimate vibration.

Ask yourself the question, 'Is this single, indivisible vibration me, or not me?' Thought tells us that we are experiencing something called a floor or a chair, or a world, made out of dead matter. But in our actual experience there is a single, seamless, indivisible vibration, made only of the knowing of it. Is there anything in our current experience other than the knowing of it?

The experience of the hand on the floor or chair is a single, seamless, indivisible experience, made only of knowing. We cannot divide that experience into a hand and a floor. As 'hand' the experience is 'me'; as 'floor' it is 'not me'. But the experience is not 'hand' and 'floor'. If we were to label this sensation we could call it 'handfloor', or 'handchair'.

Go to that experience and see if you can find an actual line that separates the hand from the floor or chair. See that the line is in thought, not experience. In reality the experience is neither hand nor floor. All that is there is pure knowing. The sensation of handfloor or handchair is a modulation of pure knowing.

If you are sitting with a friend, reach out your hand and touch your friend. If you are on your own, do this with your feeling-imagination. In both cases, the experience takes place in Consciousness, and therefore both experiences are equally real. It is for this reason that doing this contemplation in our imagination is just as powerful as doing it 'physically'.

Take some time to allow any feelings that may be generated by touching our friend to subside. It is just a sensation. Allow that sensation to be liberated from any psychology that may be attached to it. It is a single sensation. The sensation itself is not divided into two parts, a 'me' and an 'other'. There is no actual line in the experience itself that divides the sensation into two people.

Is there any part of this sensation that is not totally intimate? Is there any substance in the sensation other than the knowing of it?

Now, instead of touching your friend, look at your friend. Our experience of the so-called other is now in the form of sight rather than touch. The so-called other, the person we see, is over there, but the experience of seeing is here.

Ask yourself the question, 'Can I find a line that divides the experience of seeing into two parts, a seer and the seen, a self and an other, a there in which the seen person is taking place in contrast to a here where I am?'

See that that line is in thought, not in experience. The experience of seeing is itself intimate and indivisible. There is no seer and no seen, no self and no other, no there in contrast to here. The place we call here is not the opposite of the place we call there.

Take some time to allow your relationships to be liberated from otherness, not-me-ness. Do this not only in relationship to people but in relationship to animals and all objects. Allow the apparent otherness or not-me-ness of the world to be liberated in this contemplation.

Now, instead of either doing or imagining this with one person, freely look around your environment. Ask yourself the question, 'Is the actual experience of seeing itself ever divided into a subject that sees and an object that is seen?'

Include the experience of hearing. Does the experience of hearing ever take place over there, at a distance from myself? See if you can find a distinction between the heard sound over there and the experience of hearing here.

See clearly that all there is to the experience of sound is hearing, and hearing takes place here, where I am – not here where I, the body, am but here, the placeless place where I, Consciousness, am.

See clearly in this way that there is never any time or distance in experience itself. There is never any separation or otherness in experience itself. Distance, separation, otherness are concepts superimposed by thought onto the intimate, indivisible reality of all experience.

See that no experience has the power to divide this seamless intimacy into separate parts and selves unless we consent to give it that power. We are free to confer that power or not.

There is nothing inherent in experience itself that has the power to divide this seamless, indivisible intimacy.

Experience itself is always only one thing – or, I should say, eternally only one thing. If we look clearly, simply and honestly at our experience, all that is found there is knowing, and it is knowing that knows this knowing. In knowing's own knowing of itself, it never finds any parts, objects or selves. It finds only its own ever-present, unlimited being.

SUFFERING IS A CALL FROM LOVE

Any movement of mind towards its source is a movement away from its source. See what happens to mind when this is understood.

Attention, from the Latin *a tendere*, meaning 'to stretch towards', is a movement of Awareness towards an object. It is, as it were, a movement away from itself towards something that seems to be other than itself, the object. Therefore, Awareness cannot attend to itself – it cannot stretch itself towards itself.

If someone were to ask us, relatively speaking, 'Reach out for that cup of coffee on the table', we would reach or stretch towards the object. If someone were to say to us, 'Reach for yourself', what would we do?

We cannot go towards ourself. 'Ourself' in this context is our self of Awareness. Awareness cannot reach towards itself because it is already at itself. In other words, Awareness doesn't need to assume the form of attention or mind in order to know itself. It only needs to assume the form of attention or mind to know something that seems at first to be other than itself, such as a thought, feeling, sensation or perception. To know itself, it doesn't need to go anywhere, or reach for anything, or direct itself towards an object. It is already present in the place of itself.

This is why meditation, the ultimate meditation, is a non-practice. Any effort that we make would only be an effort towards something other than ourself.

This is why Ashtavakra said, 'For the sage even blinking is too much trouble.' For the sage, that is, for Awareness, it knows itself simply by being itself. Its being of itself *is* its knowing of itself. See what happens to mind when this is understood.

Remember, mind is not an entity; it is an activity. See what happens to the activity of mind when this is understood. No discipline: understanding alone is sufficient, experiential understanding.

The fish in the ocean believes that it is searching for water because the water is missing. In fact, the water seems to be missing *because* the fish is searching for it. The water is everywhere, but because the fish is searching for it somewhere, it seems to be nowhere.

Although Awareness is everything, because the mind is seeking it as something it seems to be nothing.

It is not because Awareness is so far that it seems to be missing; it is because it is so close, so close to itself that there is no room, no distance between itself and itself, and therefore no room for a practice or a path. Any path could only lead it from itself to an object. Having no room for a path and therefore no room for a practice, there is no room for a practitioner, a self to travel from here to there.

Meditation is between Awareness and itself. 'I am the Alpha and the Omega': I am simultaneously the origin, the path and the goal.

*   *   *

Just as attention rises from its source in Awareness and directs itself towards a thought or perception, so desire or longing rises from its source in Awareness and directs itself towards a feeling, towards a feeling of happiness, peace or love.

The source of attention we call Awareness; the source of desire or longing we call love. Attention is Awareness directed towards an object; desire is love directed towards an object. Awareness and love are two names for the same thing, one in relation to thought, the other in relation to feeling.

Just as attention seeks Awareness because it thinks that it is missing, whereas in reality it is missing because we seek it, so we feel that we desire love because it is missing. In fact, it is missing *because* we desire it. It is our longing for it that makes it seem to be absent.

In other words, what we truly long for can never be found as an object of our longing. Our very longing itself arises from that for which we long. In fact, our longing doesn't just arise from that for which we long; it is made of that for which we long.

Our longing for love, for peace, for happiness is like a current in the ocean in search of water – not just appearing in, not just arising from, but made out of the very stuff for which it is in search. This is why the Italian monk said, 'Lord, Thou art the very love with which I love Thee.'

We do not search for love because it is absent; it seems to be absent because we search for it. Our search is made out of the very stuff for which we are in search. What happens to our longing when this is understood and felt?

If the relationship in which we invested our love now seems to be missing or absent, allow the pain of that separation to gently invite your longing back to its source. The pain of separation is not on account of the absence of love; it is love itself calling our longing back to itself. The pain of separation is love calling to us, 'Come back to me. I am so close to you.'

The pain of separation is the ocean reminding the current that it is made of water.

*   *   *

Feel that our emotions are not just a single current in the ocean. The pain of separation, the feeling of shame or guilt, the sense of being unworthy or unlovable, the feeling of failure or lack, all of these are like little currents in the ocean.

All our life, we have been motivated towards objects, substances, activities, states of mind and relationships in order to avoid the discomfort of these feelings. We wouldn't be here if that had worked.

Do the opposite. Feel that you are this loving, self-aware ocean, and that all these currents are appearing in you, made of you.

Take whatever feeling or emotion is present, if indeed there are any feelings and emotions present, and turn towards it instead of away from it, as fully and intimately as you can. Be very sensitive to the slightest aversion to it. And if there are no feelings present you can just do this with the current sensation.

Take time. There is such a strong habit of aversion to these painful feelings that it takes more than one look to really, fully face and feel them. Take time. Feel the old habit of aversion: 'I can't stand the pain of separation. I can't stand the feeling of guilt or shame. I have been running from it all my life. It has dogged me all my life.' Turn round. Totally open yourself to it.

Ask yourself the question, 'Is it the pain of separation, our guilt, our shame, our sorrow that is so unbearable, or is it our resistance to it that is unbearable?'

Ask yourself the question, 'Why is the tingling sensation at the soles of my feet bearable, but the pain of separation, sorrow, guilt, shame, fear unbearable?'

Go back and forth between these two experiences. They are both equally currents in the ocean, made only of water. Don't think about this; go with your feeling-sensitivity. Don't just observe the two currents – the sensation at the soles of your feet and the pain of separation, sorrow, guilt, shame – from the outside. Go close up to each current, swim around in each current. What makes one bearable and the other unbearable, if we remove the labels, the ideas, the stories and go to the actual experience itself?

To be free of emotion is not to reject emotion or to remove ourself from it. It is to be so intimately one with it, so close to it, that there is no room for the emotion *plus* a rejection. It is to be so close to the emotion, to be so intimately one with it, that we cannot separate ourself out from it and turn round and say, 'I don't like this. This is unbearable.'

The current is never unbearable for the water. Be the water in the current. The water cannot even say 'current'. It is too close to itself to remove itself and name a current. Be so close to the emotion – to the sorrow, the shame, the guilt, the fear – so inside of it, so intimate and embracing and allowing of it, that you cannot separate yourself from it and give it a name.

This is the Tantric approach, not the Vedantic approach. We are not taking the 'I am *not* this, I am *not* this, I am *not* this' approach. We are taking the 'I *am* this, I *am* this, I *am* this' approach.

I, Awareness, am so intimately one with experience that I cannot even separate myself from it and call it experience. I cannot name it. I have no knowledge of separation, or shame, or guilt, or fear. To label experience as such we have to separate ourself from it, to look at it from a distance.

It's only when we look at experience from a distance that we can name it and thus find it unbearable.

If we want to be free of emotion, we must come closer to the emotion, so close that there is no room for resistance to arise. It is only possible to resist emotion if we place some distance between ourself and the emotion and say, 'I don't like it.' When there is no distance between the 'I' and the 'it', there is no room for resistance. See what happens to your emotion when this is the case.

*   *   *

Emotion is not transformed by this approach; its reality is revealed. The current is not transformed; it is simply revealed to be water. The only substance present in the pain of separation – our sorrow, our shame, our guilt or fear – is love itself. But we cannot know that by rejecting the emotion, by escaping from it.

If we are using our spiritual path to get rid of our suffering, then our spiritual path is just a variation of our previous, worldly path. It is just a refinement of the worldly, materialistic approach.

Do not try to get rid of your suffering. Do the opposite: draw it close. Draw it so close that you cannot even label it 'suffering' anymore. You cannot separate yourself from it and give it a name.

Be very sensitive to the old agenda of wanting to get rid of our suffering, creeping in. Be careful that we are not practising this in order to get rid of our suffering.

There is a very easy test to make sure this is not happening. We just ask ourself the question, 'Can I live with this feeling forever?' When we can answer 'Yes' to that question, we know there is no resistance to the feeling. See what happens to the feeling when we can answer 'Yes' to that question. It is not transformed; rather, its nature is revealed.

It is only possible to know what something is by separating ourself from it. It is only when we view experience from a distance, from the distance of a separate self, that we can give it a name and know it as an object. In the absence of that distance or separation, we cannot know what anything is, and therefore there is no motivation to avoid or resist.

When we are so close to experience, when we know ourself as the water in the current, when there is no room to stand back from our feelings and name them, there is no room to either like them or dislike them.

Suffering can only stand when we take a distance from our feelings. When the distance between ourself and our suffering collapses, the stuff that our suffering is made of is revealed. The pain of our separation and sorrow is revealed as love. Love is the name that is given to experience when it is divested of this sense of separation.

We cannot find love by escaping or avoiding experience, particularly painful feelings. If we want to find love in our longing, in our pain, in our sorrow, we have to go so closely up to it, to allow it so fully into ourself, that we cannot stand back and name it. We have to breathe the feeling so fully into ourself, open ourself so fully to it, that it is impossible for resistance to arise. Without resistance, how can suffering stand?

It is in this context that I say, God doesn't know our suffering. God is love. There is no separation possible in love. The water in the ocean can only know water. Water never comes in contact with anything other than itself.

KISS THE TOAD

If you find that your mind is straying from its home, not just its home in the heart of Awareness, at the background of all experience, but its home in the midst of all experience, ask yourself the question, 'Where is my mind going, and why?'

The mind is asking itself the question, 'Why are you leaving your current, direct experience and seeking in time for an alternative?' Don't answer that question yet. Just allow the mind to ask itself that question, and see what happens.

The mind is only seeking to leave the current experience because it finds something about the current experience intolerable, and therefore it is seeking to bring this uncomfortable feeling to an end by seeking in time. It may not know exactly what it is seeking. The mind will just be roaming in the past or the future for something that will alleviate whatever it is that seems to be intolerable or unpleasant about the current situation.

So become in touch with the impulse, at the level of feeling, the uncomfortable feeling or sensation which is the impulse for the mind's desire to avoid the feeling or sensation and seek in time.

Try to feel the uncomfortable feeling, if it is an emotion, or the sensation if it is physical pain, which the mind is avoiding. For instance, the sound of children is not uncomfortable or intolerable, and therefore doesn't trigger an escape from that experience; it doesn't compel us to seek in time for something that seems not to be present.

But a feeling of boredom, for instance, is intolerable. It may be a relatively mild feeling, but just the feeling of boredom is enough to trigger the mind to embark on a journey away from the current experience into time, into the past or the future. All it is seeking for in the past or the future is an object that will distract it from the discomfort of the boredom and will therefore seem to bring an end to the boredom.

The acquisition of such an object, or even the activity of seeking for it, doesn't in fact bring the boredom to an end; it simply masks it. As soon as the object or activity vanishes, the boredom will just resurface.

Don't discipline the mind. We are just getting in touch with the feeling-impulse behind or underneath much of the mind's activity.

The feeling may be a little more intense than simply boredom. It might be sorrow, or grief, or shame, or lack. All such feelings are uncomfortable or intolerable to various degrees. In order to escape the discomfort of these feelings, the mind generates thoughts that wander off into a far-off country, wander off far away from the current experience into time, looking for an object that will bring the discomfort of the feeling to an end. Even if the mind doesn't find an object, just the activity of seeking is enough to mask the discomfort of the feeling.

So, when the mind asks itself the question, 'What are you seeking, and why?', when it meets its own activity of seeking with this question, an honest mind will answer, 'I am seeking to avoid the discomfort of painful feelings or sensations. I am seeking an object, substance, state of mind or relationship which will bring this discomfort to an end.'

Confront the mind with the clear understanding that the activity of seeking, or the acquisition of an object, does not bring the discomfort of the feeling to an end; it simply masks it. As soon as the acquired object, substance, state of mind or relationship comes to an end or vanishes, the uncomfortable feeling simply resurfaces.

Most people's lives are dominated by the sole desire to avoid the discomfort of these unbearable feelings. Very often these feelings are laid down early in life, and this pattern of feeling, avoiding, seeking, briefly acquiring, feeling again, avoiding, seeking, acquiring…is a pattern that dominates most people's lives. It is the cycle of addiction, punctuated by moments of temporary release, which dominates almost all people – or I should say, dominates almost all minds.

It is, of course, this cycle of feeling, avoiding, seeking and temporary release that is the foundation of all addiction, whether our addictions are to objects and substances or whether they are more subtle, such as the addiction to thinking.

*   *   *

So, be in touch with whatever in your experience now seems to be unpleasant or intolerable, either a feeling or a sensation. If it's a feeling, it will be an emotion; if it's a sensation, it will be physical pain.

Instead of avoiding that feeling or sensation, do the opposite: go towards it, or invite it to come nearer to you, closer to you. I'm not talking about an image or a memory of a situation in your life that is difficult; I'm talking about your current experience now of a feeling or a sensation that is unpleasant.

Turn towards it; begin to draw it close. This is not a single event, but gradually drawing the feeling or sensation closer to you. You are walking into the fire of the feeling.

As the distance between you and the feeling reduces, as the feeling comes closer and closer, keep asking yourself the question, 'Can I live with this feeling forever?' That question will expose that part of your current experience that is intolerable or unpleasant. Go to that part of the current experience that is intolerable or unpleasant, and draw it closer.

Be very sensitive to your experience. Some feelings don't at first appear to be unpleasant. Grief, sorrow, loss, shame are obviously unpleasant, but take the experience of desire. Desire is, by definition, the desire for something that is not present. In other words, desire is a subtle rejection of the current experience. So, although desire may not register as an uncomfortable feeling, be very sensitive to it. It is based on the feeling that something is missing.

Don't discipline your desire; don't say, 'I shouldn't be feeling this.' On the contrary, do the opposite: feel the energy of the desire, the sense of lack that is contained in the desire, irrespective of what the desire is for. It may be sexual desire, or a desire for an object, a state of mind, any desire; bring it close. Be sensitive to the sense of lack, the sense, 'I need something to fulfil myself' at the heart of that desire. Bring that feeling close.

This is not the Vedantic approach, where we discover our true nature in the background of experience. It is the Tantric approach, in which reality is found in the midst of experience. This approach was much more fully developed in the East than it was in the West, due to the suppressive nature of the Christian religion, but it found its way into our folklore and stories.

Remember the story of the princess who had to kiss the frog before it turned into the handsome prince. She had to first kiss that which was most repulsive to her. She had to go close to that which she mostly deeply feared.

Remember *Beauty and the Beast*. Beauty was living with the Beast, and every day he asked her to marry him, and every day she said no. Every night she dreamt of a prince who asked her, 'Why do you keep saying no to me?' but she didn't realise that the prince was the Beast. She was convinced that the Beast was keeping a prince locked up somewhere in his castle.

It was only when she left the Beast's castle and went back to her sister's, and stayed away for longer than she had agreed with the Beast, that she looked into the mirror that he had given her. And she saw the Beast, heartbroken in his castle, half dead with grief from being separated from her.

So she returned to the Beast and felt compassion and love for him. As she bent over him to take care of him, one of her tears fell onto him and he was immediately transformed into the prince. She came close to that which she had spent so many years avoiding.

Bring the feeling so close that you can no longer stand back from it and give it a name, let alone a cause. It's just a nameless intensity of feeling. In other words, kiss the toad. Take the unbearable feeling in your hands. Caress it.

If there are no feelings present, just do the same thing with the current sensation, whether it is painful or neutral.

Ask yourself the question, 'Is the feeling or sensation that thought used to label sorrow, grief, loneliness, shame, or (if it's a sensation) the sensation that thought used to label pain, unbearable? Is it even unpleasant?'

If there is a trace of unpleasantness to it, it means we have not yet brought it completely close. Go to that part of the feeling that still seems to be unpleasant. Bring it closer; merge with it more intimately.

Ask yourself the question, 'If I were to name this feeling, what name would I give it?'

It is only possible to give something a name if it stands at a distance from us. We can only name an object, and to name that object we have to stand as a separate subject. If you can give your current feeling a name, it means that you have not yet brought it fully close. If it still feels like sorrow, it means you are standing apart from it as a separate self. Bring the feeling closer.

The eye cannot see itself, because there is no distance between itself and itself; therefore, it cannot see itself as an eye. The only reason we can name our feelings as sorrow, shame, loneliness is because we are standing apart from them as a separate self.

It is not the feeling that is intolerable; it is the distance between ourself and that feeling that is intolerable. The separate self *is* that distance. The separate self tries to increase the distance between itself and uncomfortable feelings by moving away from them, towards objects. But the real resolution of feelings is to do the opposite, to close the distance, to bring the feeling closer and closer and closer until, like the eye that cannot see itself, we can no longer name this feeling. We have no idea that it is sorrow or grief or loneliness. It is just an unnameable, neutral intensity.

Keep asking yourself the question from time to time, 'Is there anything unpleasant about my current experience?'

See that the unpleasantness is not in the experience itself; it is in our resistance to it. That resistance is the separate self, the distance between a self and experience, and that distance creates the subject–object relationship.

So, if there is just a tinge of unpleasantness left in your current experience, put that unpleasantness under the microscope. Bring it closer. Don't just think this; feel it. Take the unpleasantness in your hands, caress it, kiss it, open yourself fully to it, until you can say with complete honesty, 'I can live with you forever.'

*　　*　　*

Be sensitive to the slightest impulse to avoid your current experience, to leave the now.

Time is created by the impulse to avoid our current experience and replace it with something that seems not to be present. With that impulse an apparent future, in which happiness may be achieved, is created.

For so long we have been conditioned to believe that happiness is to be found by avoiding uncomfortable feelings through the acquisition of objects, substances, and so on. It is the very opposite: the happiness, peace or love that we seek is concealed at the very heart of experience. It is our rejection of uncomfortable feelings that makes the happiness that lies at their heart seem to be missing.

It is the rejection, not the feeling itself. It is the apparent unbearableness of the feeling that conceals the happiness that not only lies at its heart but is, in fact, the stuff out of which all feelings are made.

The loss of a loved one is made out of the love for which we long.

Ask yourself the question, 'Is there any distance between myself and my experience?' If there is any distance, that distance is the separate self; that distance is our suffering. It is only possible to know what experience is when it is looked at from the outside, by an observer. From the inside it is not possible to know what anything is.

The experience of love is the collapse of the imaginary distance between ourself and our experience. We all know this in relationship. The experience of love is the experience of the absence of distance between ourself and another.

Happiness is not a pleasant feeling; it is the absence of distance between ourself and our feelings. Why do unpleasant sensations make us unhappy and pleasant sensations make us happy? The only reason is that with an unpleasant sensation we are motivated to move away from it, whereas with a pleasant sensation we are attracted towards it.

In other words, in a pleasant sensation there is a merging of ourself with the sensation. There is a dissolution between the self and sensation. It is not the sensation that causes the happiness; it is the absence of distance between ourself and the sensation. It is the dissolution of the separate self that gives rise to the happiness, not the acquisition of the sensation.

This is why the French word for orgasm is *la petite mort*, a little death. It is not the sensation that brings happiness. It is that in that moment the distance between ourself and the object collapses. There is a little death of the separate self, and when the separate self disappears, the stuff out of which the sensation is made, happiness itself, shines. It is not the sensation that delivers the happiness. It is the absence of the self that reveals the ever-present, underlying happiness, the substance of all feelings.

Exactly the same is true of our perceptions. The experience of beauty is nothing to do with a particular object or perception; it is the collapse of the distinction or the distance between the object and the self. Some objects have the power to draw us closer to them: a walk in nature, a piece of music. Other perceptions we resist, and therefore they make us unhappy; we call them ugly.

The beauty is not in the object. The experience of beauty is the absence of distance between ourself and the object. The experience of ugliness is not in the object; it is the distance between ourself and the object, caused by our rejection.

Love is to relationship what happiness is to feelings, what beauty is to perception: the reality out of which all experience is made.

Beauty is not a property of objects, happiness is not a property of feelings, love is not a property of relationships. Beauty, happiness, love – these are just the common names for reality, the stuff out of which all experience is made.

It is the separating of ourself from our experience that causes beauty, happiness and love to seem to be missing. That is why the separate self is always on a search for beauty, happiness or love. The separate self can never find what it is seeking, because its own activity veils that for which it is in search. In fact, the separate self is not an entity; it is the activity of seeking.

* * *

Come back to your feelings and perceptions. Is there the slightest impulse in you to move away from the current feeling or perception? See what happens to thinking when there is not the slightest impulse to move away from the current feeling or perception.

The separate self is not an entity; it is an activity. Allow this activity to come slowly, effortlessly, naturally to rest in this disinterested contemplation of experience.

Notice that we haven't touched our experience; we haven't manipulated it or disciplined it in any way whatsoever. The disciplining of experience is the activity of the ego.

We are seeing into the heart of experience, not trying to change or manipulate it. What we seek, what we long for, lives at the heart of all experience. It can never be found by avoiding experience.

The ego lives in obscurity. If we bring experience close, go into it deeply and intimately, we never find a separate self. The separate self simply perpetuates its illusory existence by seeking happiness in objects. The activity of that seeking is made out of the stuff for which it is in search.

Is there the slightest impulse to leave the now? And if there is no impulse, where is there for thought to go?

The only place thought cannot stand is the now.

AWARENESS'S SACRIFICE OF ITS OWN ETERNITY

See clearly that our primary experience is to be aware, or Awareness itself.

Being aware, or Awareness itself, is the primary and essential ingredient of all experience.

No particular experience – that is, no particular thought, sensation or perception – is essential to experience, because all thoughts, sensations and perceptions disappear, but experience remains. Awareness itself, or the experience of being aware, is the only element of experience that is ever-present. It is the background or substratum upon which all experience plays.

When I say that being aware, or Awareness itself, is 'our' primary experience I imply that there is a 'we', or an 'I', that has the experience of being aware, and in that sense the phrase is misleading. 'I' is not an entity that *has* the experience of being aware; 'I' *is* the experience of being aware, or Awareness itself.

So when we say being aware, or Awareness itself, is our primary experience, what is really meant is that being aware, or Awareness itself, is Awareness's primary experience. Before Awareness is aware of any thing, it is simply aware of itself; it is simply present and aware, without being aware of any thing.

Awareness's simple awareness of itself is the experience that shines in each of our finite minds as the knowledge 'I am' or 'I am aware'. In other words, each of our finite minds has access to its essential reality through the experience 'I am' or 'I am aware'.

That is why the first stage of the spiritual path involves this tracing back of the attention from what we are aware *of* to the experience of being aware itself.

Now, when I say 'the tracing back of the attention', I don't mean to imply that the experience of being aware, or Awareness itself, can ever be found as an object of our attention. The experience of being aware is the subject or source of attention. What is sometimes called the tracing back of our attention is more like a sinking back or a relaxation of the focus of our attention from objects.

We could say, 'Feel the presence of Awareness in the background of all experience'. Again, that is not quite right, because Awareness can never be felt, but within the limitations of language it is a legitimate thing to say. Even more accurate would be simply, 'Be knowingly this Presence in the background of experience, or this aware field in which experience appears'. Let your mind relax back into that. Let your mind sink deeper and deeper into its source of simply being aware.

*　　*　　*

Notice that absolutely no effort is required to be the Awareness that we essentially are.

All experience arises in this field of Awareness. All experience is known by it and is made of it. It is Awareness itself that assumes the forms of everything that appears within it, just like the screen itself assumes the forms of all the images that appear on it.

Prior to the appearance of experience, Awareness is an empty field, an empty field of infinite possibility. Because it has no name or form of its own, it has the capacity within it to assume the form of all names and forms. Because the screen is colourless, it can appear as any colour.

Because the essential nature of Awareness is empty of all names and forms, there are no divisions within it; it is a seamless, indivisible field. As such, it is said to be infinite, that is, not finite. Anything that is finite must have a border, an edge, a name and a form; it must be limited. The empty field of being aware, or Awareness itself, is without names and forms, without limits. There are no parts within it, thus it is said to be infinite.

The reason I take care to explain in an experiential way what the word 'infinite' means is so that we don't think, 'Oh, infinite Awareness, that sounds amazing. I could never know that', and to make it clear that what I am describing, the description of Awareness as infinite, is based on our current, direct experience of being aware. It is not a special or magical knowledge that I have access to that you cannot know. I have no more access to my true nature of Awareness than you do.

Likewise, the experience of being aware, or Awareness itself, is the ever-present background of all experience. It never experiences itself appearing or disappearing. The states of waking, dreaming and sleeping appear and disappear on it or in it, just like the news, the drama and the documentary appear sequentially on the screen, but the screen doesn't appear and disappear sequentially. It is not in time.

Awareness is not in time; it is eternally present to its own being. That is why it is said to be eternal: ever-present now. Again, I take care and time to explain this so that when we hear that Awareness is eternal, we don't think that the teaching is talking about some marvellous, abstract philosophical idea that we don't have access to. It is our own intimate experience, that is, it is Awareness's own intimate experience, that it is ever-present. Awareness has never had the experience of itself appearing or disappearing. In other words, it has no knowledge or experience of its own birth or death.

Awareness doesn't have to be made infinite and eternal; it simply has to be relieved of the superimposed beliefs and feelings that make it seem to be temporary and finite. The superimposed feelings and beliefs that make Awareness seem to be temporary and finite come from the 'I, Awareness, am identical to the body' belief.

When Awareness seems to shrink itself inside the body, it seems to lose the knowledge of its own eternal, infinite nature, and seems instead to acquire the temporary, finite qualities of the body. When the body is born it seems that Awareness is born. If the body is male or female, Awareness seems to be male or female. As the body grows old, it seems as if Awareness is growing old. When a sensation called loneliness appears, it seems that I, Awareness, am lonely. When the body approaches death, it seems that I, Awareness, am going to die. And although Awareness has never experienced the disappearance of itself, most of us still believe that when the body dies, I, Awareness, am going to die with it.

*   *   *

However, this 'Awareness in the body' entity, which is sometimes called the ego or separate self, is not a mistake. It is a function through which Awareness is able to know or realise a segment or section of its infinite potential.

Manifestation means form, and form means limitation. In order for infinite, formless Awareness to manifest a limited form, or collection of forms – that is, the world – it must give up the knowing of its own infinite being. It must sacrifice the knowledge of its own eternity in order to know anything other than its own infinite self. In order to know a finite object, it must seem to become a temporary subject.

In order to bring forth manifestation out of itself, infinite, indivisible Awareness must seem to divide itself into two parts: a subject and an object, a knower and a known. That is why we always seem to experience the world from a limited point of view. Even when we have a dream at night, in order to know the dreamed world we have to become a person in that dreamed world, from which it is known or seen.

If Mary, asleep in Buckland Hall, wants to know the streets of New York, she has to overlook the knowing of her own limitless, indivisible mind and seem to become Jane on the streets of New York. It is only as Jane's apparently finite mind that Mary's infinite mind is able to experience the streets of New York.

From Mary's point of view, Jane's inside experience of thoughts and feelings, and her outside experience, the streets of New York, are all equally a manifestation of her own indivisible mind. But from Jane's point of view, her experience is divided into a self on the inside, made of mind, and a world on the outside, made of matter.

Jane, walking the streets of New York, becomes a scientist at Columbia University, and she devotes her whole life to exploring the nature of matter. She never discovers it, because in order to discover the nature of her experience, she has to discover the nature of her own mind, which experiences it. That is why physicists in our culture still don't know what matter is made of: very few of them are willing to explore the nature of their own minds.

If Jane turns her attention towards the nature of her own mind, it leads her backwards, away from the objects that she has been studying, towards the subject of experience. And if she is devoted, if she is deeply interested in the nature of her own experience and traces her mind back far enough, she realises that her finite mind is simply a modulation of Mary's infinite mind. Jane realises that the knowing with which she knows her experience is itself unlimited, infinite.

In other words, Jane has to trace her experience back in the opposite direction. Mary's mind went in one direction, assumed the form of Jane's mind in order to know Jane's world. Jane now has to travel back in the opposite direction to know the nature of that world.

That is why in the Tantric tradition they say, 'The path by which we came is the path by which we return.'

*   *   *

So, just allow your mind to sink deeper and deeper into the simple experience of being aware.

Notice that when any experience appears, that is, all thinking, feeling, sensing and perceiving, it appears as a colouring of Awareness. Just as the screen colours itself to appear as the image, so being aware colours itself in the forms of thinking, sensing and perceiving. As thinking, sensing and perceiving, Awareness itself seems to appear as a multiplicity and diversity of objects, and it seems to know those objects from the point of view of a separate subject.

Just as a screen seems to veil itself by appearing as the image, so when Awareness itself takes the form of manifestation, it seems to lose itself in its manifestation. Awareness gives birth to the world from within itself and then seems to become lost in that world as a separate knower.

Now, there are some experiences that the separate knower has – that is, Jane on the streets of New York has – which seem to have the power to convince the separate knower of its separateness. Experiences of loneliness, sorrow, jealously, shame, and so on, seem to convince the separate self that it is indeed a separate self. But there are other experiences that the separate self has – that Jane on the streets of New York has – that seem to awaken in her the memory of her true nature. When she goes north at the weekends and walks in the countryside, she notices that there is a relaxation of her mind, and as her mind relaxes, its background is felt. She feels that as the experience of peace or beauty.

Of course, to begin with, she's a scientist, so she just dismisses the experience of peace as an irrelevant, subjective experience. And yet, strangely, she finds herself drawn more and more to such experiences. She notices that some of her experiences have the capacity to increase her sense of separation, but she notices that there are other experiences – certain friends, walking in nature, certain exhibitions or concerts – that have a kind of power in them to relax and expand her mind and give her access to this peace in the background of experience.

Wind blowing

Listen to the sound of the wind. It is just the faintest colouring of Awareness. It is like the palest of watercolour washes over the white page of Awareness, with almost no capacity at all to veil its background. In fact, the translucency of the sound seems to shine with the silence of its background.

Listen to the sound of the wind when its colour begins to get a little more intense.

Flute playing

And see that when the sound disappears, all that has disappeared is a colouring of the experience of being aware. The stuff out of which the sound is made hasn't disappeared; it has just ceased colouring itself in the form of a sound.

Flute playing

When the sound is absent, the knowing with which the sound is known is still present. When the sound is present, all there is to the sound is the knowing of it. When the sound disappears, that knowing doesn't disappear; it just loses a temporary name and form.

So, in the transition now from silence to sound, see that no new substance comes into experience. Now there is knowing, and when the sound appears there is nothing else in your experience other than knowing. It is just that this knowing colours itself and assumes the form of the sound.

Flute playing

Some objects – nature, works of art, the expressions of the teaching – have a power within them to expand or dissolve the mind and reveal its essential nature, whereas other objects or experiences seem to confirm the finite mind in its belief and feeling of separation. However, in reality, all objects, all experiences shine only with the light of their background. No image has the capacity to veil the screen any more than any other image, unless we give it permission to do so.

Before any experience tells us anything about a world made out of matter, or a mind made out of thoughts and feelings, it tells us first about the presence of Awareness. Every object and experience, irrespective of its content, shines primarily with its own existence. Every object asserts, 'Here I am', irrespective of its content. The 'isness' of each experience belongs to infinite Consciousness. It *is* infinite Consciousness.

No object or experience has the capacity to veil Awareness unless we give it permission to do so, in which case it will conform with the permission we give it.

*   *   *

Notice, when the sound appears again, that it appears within this limitless field. It is not put in from the outside; it arises within the field and is a modulation of the field.

Flute playing

And when the sound disappears, ask yourself the question, 'Where has it gone?'

How can something become nothing? If it was something then, and has become nothing now, what happened to its somethingness? And if it was nothing before it became something, where did its somethingness come from?

How can something that appears in time arise out of that which is timeless?

Shakespeare said, 'And as imagination bodies forth the forms of things unknown, a poet's pen turns to shape them, and gives to airy nothing a local habitation and a name.'

He might have said, 'And as imagination bodies forth the forms of things unknown, a musician's breath breathes to give them shape, to give them sound, and gives to airy nothing a local habitation and a name.'

It is infinite Awareness itself which freely assumes the form of the finite mind and, in doing so, brings time into existence out of eternity.

When we open our eyes, infinite Awareness assumes the form of the finite mind, in the form of perception, and brings space out of infinity into existence.

Flute playing

William Blake said, 'Every bird that cuts the airy way is an immense world of delight enclosed by the five senses.' Every bird that flies through the sky is an immense world of delight, enclosed by the five senses. Every sound that flows through Awareness is God's infinite being, shining in the form of the finite mind.

Every experience is God's infinite being, freely assuming the form of the finite mind in order to reveal a segment of its infinite potential, but in doing so it never is, knows or becomes anything other than itself.

Everything is the shining of God's infinite being.

PUBLICATIONS BY RUPERT SPIRA

The Transparency of Things – Contemplating the Nature of Experience

Presence, Volume I – The Art of Peace and Happiness

Presence, Volume II – The Intimacy of All Experience

The Ashes of Love – Sayings on the Essence of Non-Duality

The Light of Pure Knowing – Thirty Meditations on the Essence of Non-Duality

Transparent Body, Luminous World – The Tantric Yoga of Sensation and Perception

The Nature of Consciousness – Essays on the Unity of Mind and Matter

Being Aware of Being Aware – The Essence of Meditation Series, Volume I

A Meditation on I Am

The Essential Self – Three Meditations

Being Myself – The Essence of Meditation Series, Volume II

You Are the Happiness You Seek – Uncovering the Awareness of Being

Naked, Self-Aware Being – A Seven-Day Retreat in New York

An Introduction to Non-Duality, Volume I – The Recognition of Our Essential Nature

An Introduction to Non-Duality, Volume II – The Recognition of the Nature of Reality

I Am Always I

The Heart of Prayer – The Essence of Meditation Series, Volume III

The Place of Refuge – Seven Meditations

The Way of Surrender – A Weekend Retreat

The Essence of Tantra – A Weekend Retreat

The True Friend – Eight Meditations

From an early age Rupert Spira was deeply interested in the nature of reality. At the age of seventeen he learnt to meditate, and began a twenty-year period of study and practice in the classical Advaita Vedanta tradition under the guidance of Dr. Francis Roles and Shantananda Saraswati, the Shankaracharya of the north of India.

During this time he immersed himself in the teachings of P. D. Ouspensky, Krishnamurti, Rumi, Ramana Maharshi, Nisargadatta and Robert Adams, until he met his teacher, Francis Lucille, in 1997. Francis introduced Rupert to the Direct Path teachings of Atmananda Krishna Menon, the Tantric tradition of Kashmir Shaivism (which he had received from his teacher, Jean Klein), and, more importantly, directly indicated to him the true nature of experience. Rupert lives in the UK and holds regular meetings and retreats in Europe and the USA.

www.rupertspira.com

Printed in Great Britain
by Amazon

41956638R00142